"WE HAVE IT DAMN HARD OUT HERE"

"We Have It Damn Hard Out Here"

The Civil War Letters
of Sergeant Thomas W. Smith,
6th Pennsylvania Cavalry

EDITED BY

ERIC J. WITTENBERG

THE KENT STATE UNIVERSITY PRESS

Kent, Ohio, & London

©1999 by The Kent State University Press, Kent, Ohio 44242
All rights reserved
Library of Congress Catalog Card Number 98-44154
ISBN 0-87338-623-x
Manufactured in the United States of America

05 04 03 02 01 00 99   5 4 3 2 1

Library of Congress Cataloging-in-Publication Data
Smith, Thomas W., 1838?–1896.
We have it damn hard out here : the Civil War letters of Sergeant
Thomas W. Smith, 6th Pennsylvania Cavalry / edited by Eric J.
Wittenberg.
p.   cm.
Includes bibliographical references and index.
ISBN 0-87338-623-x (alk. paper) ∞
1. Smith, Thomas W., 1838?–1896—Correspondence.   2. United
States. Army. Pennsylvania Cavalry Regiment, 6th (1861–1865)
3. United States—History—Civil War, 1861–1865—Regimental
histories.   4. Pennsylvania—History—Civil War, 1861–1865—
Regimental histories.   5. United States—History—Civil War,
1861–1865—Personal narratives.   6. Pennsylvania—History—Civil
War, 1861–1865—Personal narratives.   7. United States—History—
Civil War, 1861–1865—Cavalry operations.   8. Pennsylvania—
History—Civil War, 1861–1865—Cavalry operations.   9. Soldiers—
Pennsylvania—Philadelphia—Correspondence.   10. Philadelphia
(Penn.)—Biography.   I. Wittenberg, Eric J., 1961– .   II. Title.
E527.6 6th.s65   1999
973.7'448—dc21   98-44154

British Library Cataloging-in-Publication data are available.

This book is dedicated to those who answered to the bugle call "Mount Up!"; to those who cherish the memory of the 6th Pennsylvania Cavalry; and to my long-suffering but much-loved wife, Susan Skilken Wittenberg, for her endless patience with my addiction to the Civil War.

The principal value of cavalry is derived from its rapidity and mobility. To these characteristics may be added its impetuosity, but we must be careful lest a false application be made of the last.

Lt. Gen. Antoine Henri Baron de Jomini,
Summary of the Art of War (1838)

In one respect a cavalry charge is very like ordinary life. So long as you are all right, firmly in your saddle, your horse in hand, and well armed, lots of enemies will give you a wide berth. But as soon as you have lost a stirrup, had a rein cut, have dropped your weapon, are wounded, or your horse is wounded, then is the moment from all quarters enemies rush upon you.

Sir Winston S. Churchill, *The River War* (1899)

. . . the successful cavalryman must educate himself to say "CHARGE."
I say educate himself, for the man is not born who can say it out of hand. . . .

Civilization has affected us; we abhor personal encounter. . . . We have been taught to restrain our emotions, to look upon anger as low, until many of us have never experienced the God sent ecstasy of unbridled wrath. We have never felt our eyes screw up, our temples throb and had the red mist gather in our sight.

And we expect that a man . . . shall [suddenly throw off] all caution and hurl himself on the enemy, a frenzied beast, lusting to probe his foeman's guts with three feet of steel or shatter his brains with a bullet. . . . It cannot be done—not without mental practice.

Therefore, you must school yourself to savagery. You must imagine how it will feel when your sword hilt crashes into the breastbone of your enemy. You must picture the wild exultation of the mounted charge when the lips draw back in a snarl and the voice cracks with passion. . . .

When you have acquired the ability to develop on necessity momentary and calculated savagery, you can keep your . . . clarity of vision with which the sense to calculate the chances of whether to charge or fight on foot, and having decided on the former, the magic word will transform you temporarily into a frenzied brute. . . .

To sum-up, then, you must be: a horse master; a scholar; a high minded gentleman; a cold blooded hero; a hot blooded savage. At one and the same time you must be a wise man and a fool. You must not get fat or mentally old, and you must be a personal LEADER.

George S. Patton, Jr., "The Cavalryman" (1921)

Contents

Acknowledgments and Editorial Notes

I FIRST DISCOVERED THE 6th Pennsylvania Cavalry, also known as Rush's Lancers, in 1992 while researching a biography of Gen. John Buford, the Army of the Potomac's great cavalry chieftain. My studies of this regiment's accomplishments intrigued me as I continued my research. In my quest to learn more, I discovered the letters of Sgt. Thomas W. Smith of Company I of the Lancers in the Historical Society of Pennsylvania in Smith's native Philadelphia. These sixty-seven letters provide rare insight into the workings and daily life of a noncommissioned officer in one of the Army of the Potomac's best cavalry regiments. They are filled with humor and humanity and amply demonstrate the hardships withstood by the common soldier of the Civil War. I decided to use his own words to tell the story of a young man's service in the greatest adventure of his life.

While Tom Smith was by no means an unintelligent man, he was obviously not highly educated. His letters are filled with misspellings and grammatical errors. I have maintained the misspellings and grammatical errors in order to maintain the essence and integrity of his letters. Further, I have kept his paragraphing intact, even though there are places where his paragraph breaks make poor transitions.

The only significant editorial changes I have made to Smith's letters are to silently introduce punctuation to make reading them easier. I have added periods in Smith's sentences to break up long paragraphs. Sometimes Smith used commas in inappropriate places, and I have removed a few.

I have added narrative so that the reader can make sense of Smith's letters and provided annotations to assist the reader in identifying the persons and events he describes. Occasionally I have added a word or two to the letters to clarify Smith's meaning. In those places, the changes appear in brackets [ ]. I alone am responsible for any errors in the transcription of these letters.

Finally, since Smith wrote home to his family, his letters are filled with references to family, friends, and fellow soldiers. Most of the time he referred to these people by their first names. Despite my best efforts, I have been unable to identify all of the people whom he mentions. If an endnote states "unable to identify," I was unable to determine the identity of the person Smith refers to in his letter. However, the majority of these people, particularly Smith's comrades in arms, are identified in the endnotes.

As with every project of this magnitude, many people contributed to its success, and I hope that I remember to thank everyone who provided me with assistance. If I forget someone, I sincerely hope that I will be forgiven.

The first and perhaps most significant note of gratitude must go to my friend and researcher extraordinaire Steve L. Zerbe, who did much of the basic research for this book. I also owe a particular debt of gratitude to the archivists at the Historical Society of Pennsylvania for granting me permission to publish these letters and to utilize other portions of the society's vast collection of Civil War materials. Also, Dr. Richard Sommers and David Keough of the United States Army Military History Institute at Carlisle Barracks and Randy Hackenberg of the institute's photographic section assisted me in locating research material and photographs to improve my manuscript. Dr. Richard A. Sauers allowed me to tap into his vast knowledge of an underutilized resource, the National Tribune, and also gave me leads on other good material on Rush's Lancers that appeared in several different Pennsylvania newspapers during the Civil War. Paul Birkhead combed the National Archives to obtain for me copies of service and pension records of the men of the 6th Pennsylvania Cavalry.

Clark B. "Bud" Hall, the official historian of the great Battle of Brandy Station, reviewed this manuscript and provided me with guidance. Robert F. O'Neill, Jr., of Stafford, Virginia, the foremost expert on the cavalry battles at Aldie, Middleburg, and Upperville, and the role of the Federal cavalry during the 1862 Peninsula campaign, also reviewed the manuscript and gave me good suggestions as to how to improve it. Brian C. Pohanka, noted Civil War historian, provided excellent editorial guidance and granted me permission to use a previously unpublished image of Clement Biddle Barclay, the political patron of the 6th Pennsylvania Cavalry. Terry Johnston of Clemson, South Carolina, read three different drafts of the manuscript and gave me many helpful editorial tips. Dennis Lawrence of Kansas City, Kansas, and Professor Ernie Butner were both generous with their time. Dr. Jack Welsh, of Oklahoma City, Oklahoma, provided me with necessary and insightful information on the symptoms and treatment of malaria during the Civil War. Thomas A. Canfield, who faithfully reenacts the Lancers, drew the maps and gave me the insight that helped me better understand the life and lot of the enlisted men in a Federal cavalry unit.

In addition, I must say a special thank you to my wonderful wife, Susan Skilken Wittenberg, who traveled with me to research this book and who demonstrated endless patience with my addiction to the Civil War. Without her love and support, this work would never have been possible.

Finally, I owe a special debt of gratitude to all of those who still hear the sound of the cannon's thunder and the blare of the bugles as they call "Mount Up!" To the men of the 6th Pennsylvania Cavalry, and to those who study and reenact their exploits today, I owe much gratitude.

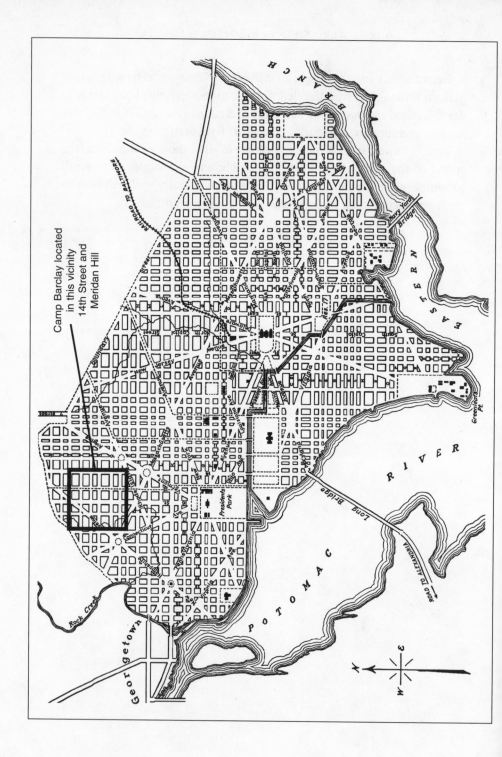

Camp Barclay located in this vicinity 14th Street and Meridan Hill

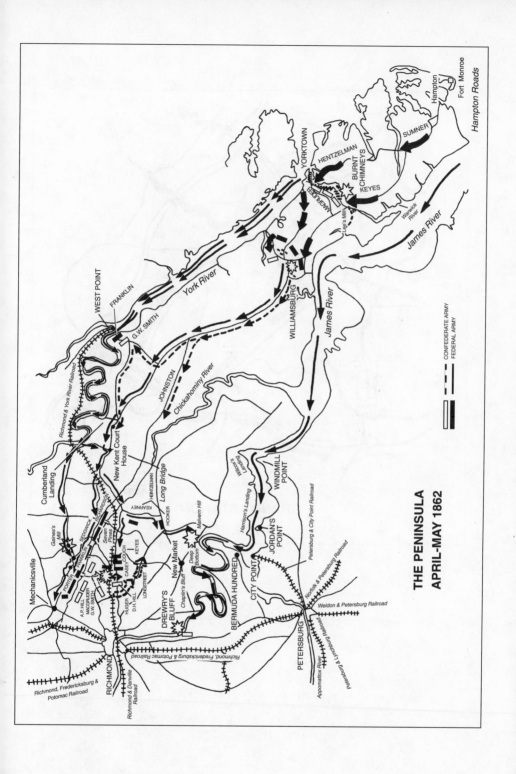

**THE PENINSULA
APRIL–MAY 1862**

CONFEDERATE ARMY
FEDERAL ARMY

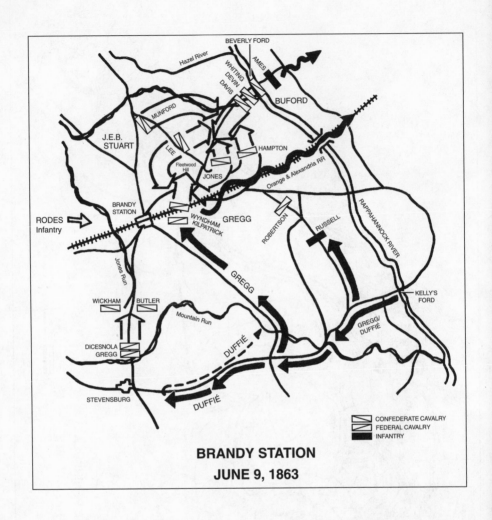

BRANDY STATION
JUNE 9, 1863

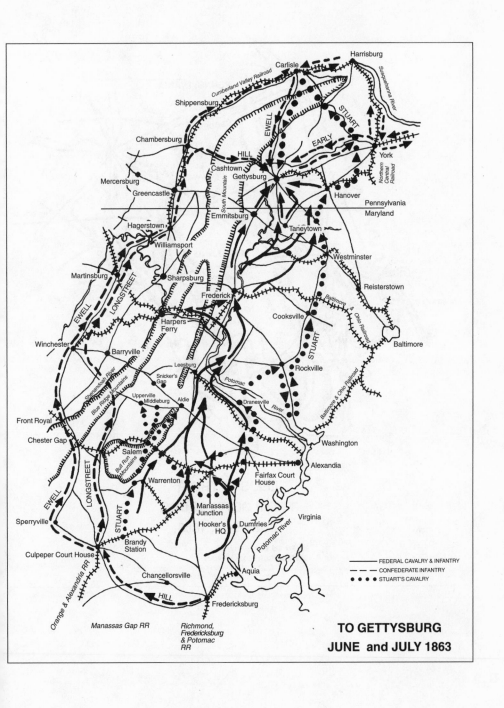

Harrisburg

Carlisle

Cumberland Valley Railroad

Shippensburg

Susquehanna River

Chambersburg

EWELL

STUART

EARLY

HILL

Cashtown

York

Mercersburg

Gettysburg

Northern Central Railroad

Greencastle

South Mountain

Hanover

Emmitsburg

Pennsylvania

Maryland

Hagerstown

Taneytown

Williamsport

Westminster

Martinsburg

Sharpsburg

Frederick

Reisterstown

EWELL

LONGSTREET

Baltimore & Ohio Railroad

Harpers
Ferry

Cooksville

Baltimore

Winchester

Barryville

STUART

Shenandoah River

Leesburg

Rockville

Snicker's
Gap

Potomac

Front Royal

Blue Ridge Mountains

Upperville
Middleburg

Aldie

Dranesville

River

Baltimore & Ohio Railroad

Chester Gap

Salem

Washington

LONGSTREET

Bull Run Mountains

Warrenton

Alexandria

Fairfax Court
House

EWELL

STUART

Manassas
Junction

Virginia

Sperryville

Hooker's
HQ

Dumfries

Potomac River

Culpeper Court House

Brandy
Station

Orange & Alexandria RR

Chancellorsville

Aquia

FEDERAL CAVALRY & INFANTRY
CONFEDERATE INFANTRY
STUART'S CAVALRY

HILL

Fredericksburg

Manassas Gap RR

Richmond,
Fredericksburg
& Potomac
RR

TO GETTYSBURG

JUNE and JULY 1863

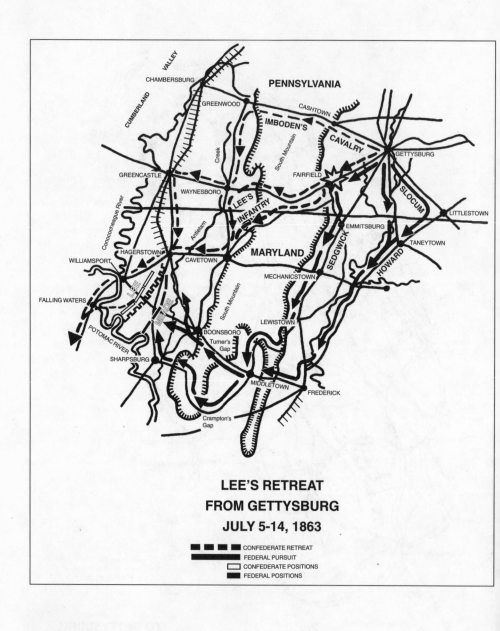

LEE'S RETREAT
FROM GETTYSBURG
JULY 5-14, 1863

CONFEDERATE RETREAT
FEDERAL PURSUIT
CONFEDERATE POSITIONS
FEDERAL POSITIONS

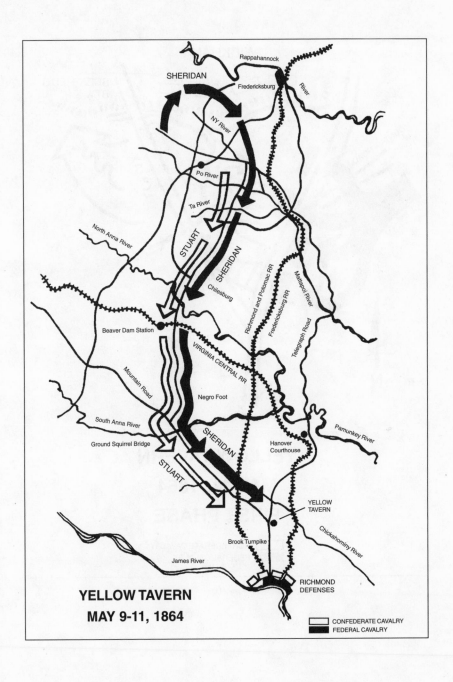

Rappahannock

SHERIDAN

Fredericksburg

River

NY River

Po River

Ta River

North Anna River

STUART

SHERIDAN

Chilesburg

Richmond and Potomac RR

Fredericksburg RR

Mattapol River

Telegraph Road

Beaver Dam Station

VIRGINIA CENTRAL RR

Mountain Road

Negro Foot

South Anna River

Ground Squirrel Bridge

SHERIDAN

STUART

Hanover
Courthouse

Pamunkey River

YELLOW
TAVERN

Brook Turnpike

Chickahominy River

James River

RICHMOND
DEFENSES

YELLOW TAVERN

MAY 9-11, 1864

CONFEDERATE CAVALRY
FEDERAL CAVALRY

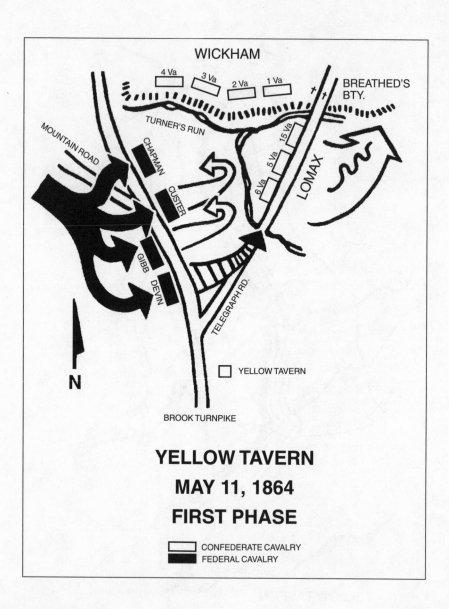

WICKHAM

4 Va 3 Va 2 Va 1 Va

BREATHED'S
BTY.

TURNER'S RUN

MOUNTAIN ROAD

CHAPMAN

CUSTER

GIBB

DEVIN

15 Va

5 Va

6 Va

LOMAX

TELEGRAPH RD.

N

YELLOW TAVERN

BROOK TURNPIKE

YELLOW TAVERN

MAY 11, 1864

FIRST PHASE

CONFEDERATE CAVALRY
FEDERAL CAVALRY

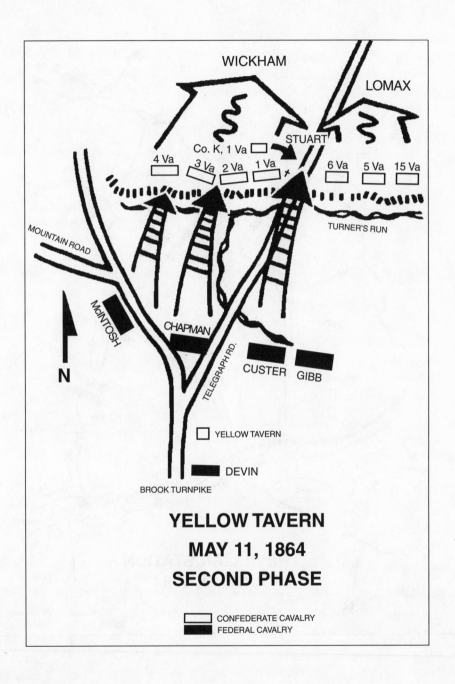

WICKHAM

LOMAX

Co. K, 1 Va

STUART

4 Va   3 Va   2 Va   1 Va

6 Va   5 Va   15 Va

MOUNTAIN ROAD

TURNER'S RUN

McINTOSH

CHAPMAN

TELEGRAPH RD.

CUSTER   GIBB

N

YELLOW TAVERN

DEVIN

BROOK TURNPIKE

YELLOW TAVERN

MAY 11, 1864

SECOND PHASE

☐ CONFEDERATE CAVALRY
■ FEDERAL CAVALRY

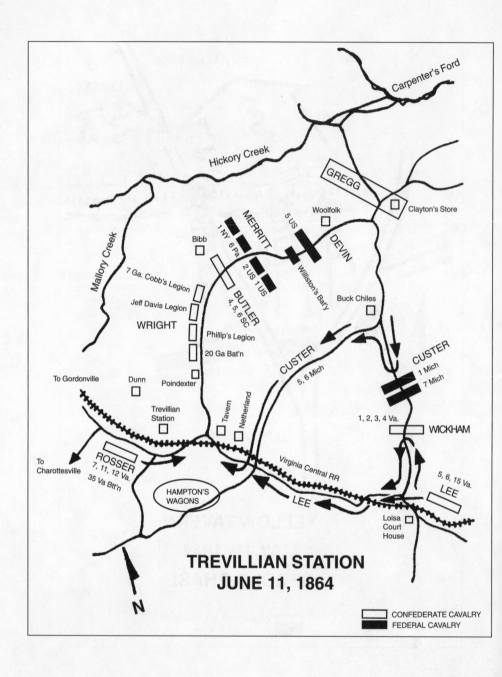

Carpenter's Ford

Hickory Creek

GREGG

Woolfolk

Clayton's Store

MERRITT

5 US

DEVIN

1 NY 6 Pa

Bibb

2 US 1 US

Williston's Bat'y

Buck Chiles

Mallory Creek

7 Ga. Cobb's Legion

Jeff Davis Legion

WRIGHT

BUTLER

4, 5, 6 SC

Phillip's Legion

20 Ga Bat'n

CUSTER

5, 6 Mich

CUSTER

1 Mich

7 Mich

To Gordonville

Dunn

Poindexter

Trevillian
Station

Tavern

Netherland

1, 2, 3, 4 Va.

WICKHAM

To
Charottesville

ROSSER

7, 11, 12 Va.

35 Va Btt'n

HAMPTON'S
WAGONS

Virginia Central RR

LEE

5, 6, 15 Va.

LEE

Loisa
Court
House

**TREVILLIAN STATION
JUNE 11, 1864**

N

| | CONFEDERATE CAVALRY |
| | FEDERAL CAVALRY |

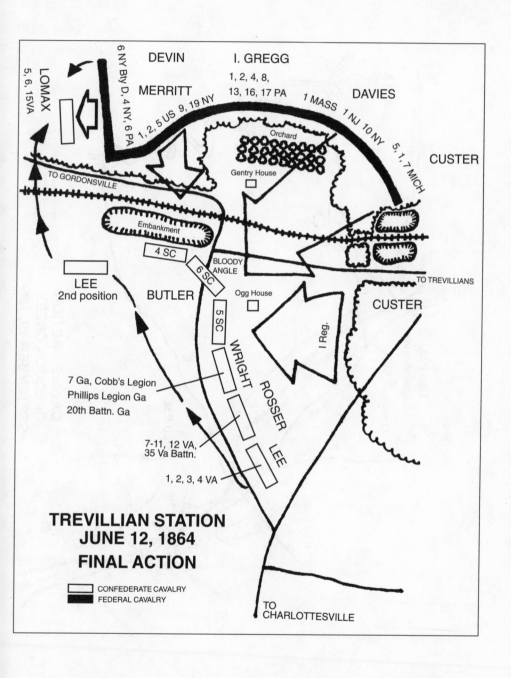

TREVILLIAN STATION
JUNE 12, 1864
FINAL ACTION

□ CONFEDERATE CAVALRY
■ FEDERAL CAVALRY

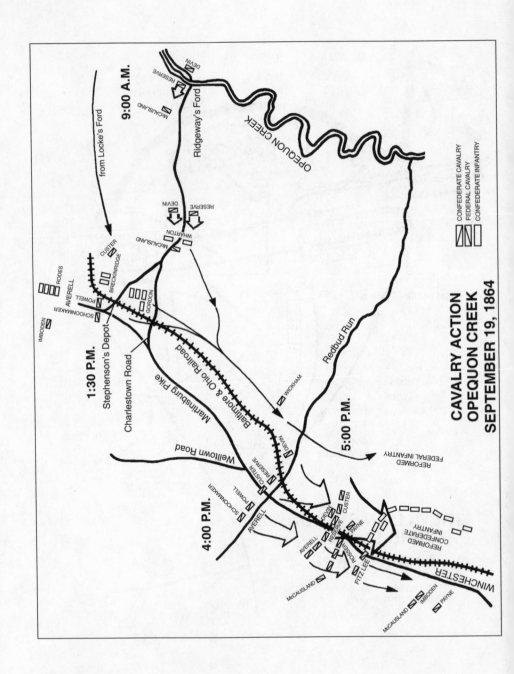

CAVALRY ACTION
OPEQUON CREEK
SEPTEMBER 19, 1864

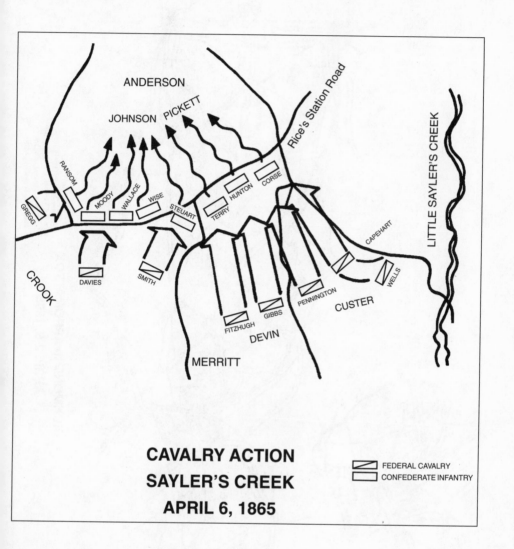

ANDERSON

JOHNSON PICKETT

Rice's Station Road

LITTLE SAYLER'S CREEK

RANSOM

GREGG

MOODY WALLACE WISE STEUART TERRY HUNTON CORSE

CAPEHART

CROOK

DAVIES SMITH

FITZHUGH GIBBS PENNINGTON WELLS

CUSTER

DEVIN

MERRITT

CAVALRY ACTION
SAYLER'S CREEK
APRIL 6, 1865

FEDERAL CAVALRY
CONFEDERATE INFANTRY

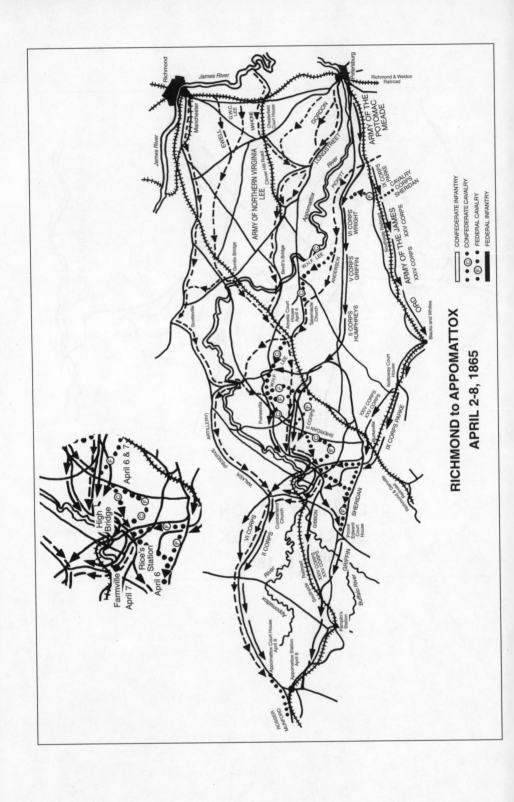

RICHMOND to APPOMATTOX
APRIL 2-8, 1865

"WE HAVE IT DAMN HARD OUT HERE"

Introduction

THIS IS THE STORY OF Sgt. Thomas W. Smith's service in the Civil War. It is also the story of his regiment, the 6th Pennsylvania Cavalry, known as Rush's Lancers, named both for the distinctive wooden lances they carried for the first two years of the war and for their first commanding officer, Col. Richard H. Rush. In order to understand Smith's story and his perspective on the American Civil War, the reader also must know the story of the Lancers, for the two stories are, inevitably, inseparable.

When the Civil War broke out, a wave of patriotic fervor crashed over the city of Philadelphia. In the opening months of the war, forty-one regiments of infantry, five batteries of artillery, and twelve regiments of cavalry were formed, with the men signing up for three year terms of service. Nearly one hundred thousand men answered the initial calls for volunteers.[1] The 6th Pennsylvania was formed in Philadelphia during the late summer and early fall of 1861 as one of the state's first contributions to the Civil War. The men represented both major political parties, although more of them were Republicans than Democrats.[2] Many of its officers had served in an elite militia unit called the First Troop Philadelphia City Cavalry, an organization that traced its roots to the American Revolution. The original First City Troop, as it was known during the Revolution, served as George Washington's bodyguard. The next generation of troopers served with distinction during the War of 1812.

The regiment's political patron was Clement Biddle Barclay, a member of the prominent Biddle and Barclay families of Philadelphia and New York. Barclay, a member of the First City Troop, had great political influence with Pennsylvania governor Andrew Gregg Curtin, serving as his unofficial aide and as goodwill ambassador to the troops. Barclay used his considerable influence to assist in forming, organizing, and outfitting this new regiment, raised money to aid in arming it, and used his fortune to look after the comfort of its troops.[3]

At age thirty-seven, Col. Richard H. Rush was a good choice to command the new regiment: He graduated with West Point's legendary class of 1846, along with fellow Philadelphians George B. McClellan and John Gibbon, Virginians Thomas Jonathan "Stonewall" Jackson, Ambrose Powell Hill, and George E. Pickett, as well as a number of other officers who achieved the rank of general during the Civil War.[4] Rush was also a grandson of Benjamin Rush of Philadelphia, a signer of both the Declaration of Independence and the Constitution, and the son of the U.S. minister to England's Court of St. James.

He was a veteran of the Mexican War and was well respected for his service in the artillery during his career in the Regular Army. By 1861, Rush had earned "an enviable reputation as a cavalry officer of the regular service."[5] Responding to President Lincoln's initial call for volunteers, Rush sought a commission as a brigadier general and command of the Commonwealth of Pennsylvania's volunteer artillery units. One of his supporters wrote, "Rush is not only in every aspect highly qualified for the command, but a gentleman of high tone, calculated to raise the character of the troops under his lead, if to reflect more honor on the state than the office can confer upon him."[6] Another soldier recalled, "Col. Rush was an excellent organizer and instructor, having but few superiors, if any. . . . He was well versed in all the requirements of the Quartermaster, Commissary and Ordinance Departments. . . . His memory was excellent; he could call every member in the regiment by name. He was exacting as to neatness and a quick appreciation of the qualities necessary for an ideal soldier."[7]

Despite these qualifications, Rush's application was rejected. Instead, Governor Curtin authorized him to raise a cavalry regiment, which would become known as either the 70th Regiment of Pennsylvania Volunteers or the 6th Pennsylvania Cavalry. Rush was mustered into the 6th Pennsylvania Cavalry on October 5, 1861, for a term of three years. He immediately set about organizing and outfitting his regiment, personally recruited most of the 750 members of the regiment, and appointed many of his own officers.[8] Tested in battle, this regiment proved to be one of the elite cavalry units on either side of the conflict.

Among the officers were twenty-five-year-old Maj. Robert Morris, Jr., a great grandson of the financier of the American Revolution; Capt. George G. Meade, Jr., son of the eventual commander of the Army of the Potomac; Capt. Charles E. Cadwalader, scion of one of Philadelphia's most influential families; Lt. Frederick C. Newhall, who would write several important historical accounts of the regiment's service; Lt. Thomas Gregg, cousin of the governor, and younger brother of Brig. Gen. David M. Gregg, who commanded a division of the Army of the Potomac's Cavalry Corps for much of the war. They also included Capt. Henry C. Whelan, who would leave behind a stirring personal account of his participation in the great cavalry battle of Brandy Station fought on June 9, 1863. Counting young George Meade, five officers from the Lancers would serve as staff officers at the Army of the Potomac's headquarters. More of Maj. Gen. George G. Meade's staff officers came from the Lancers than from any other regiment.[9] Most of these dashing young men were college educated, and many were graduates of the University of Pennsylvania.

While some of the members of the regiment had served in the Philadelphia City Troop, most of the recruits were raw city boys, unaccustomed to riding and caring for horses. Nearly all of them had to learn their trade—including how to care for their horses and how to execute difficult weapons drills—before they could even consider venturing into the field. Unlike most of their comrades in the mounted service, the men of the 6th Pennsylvania were armed with lances, weapons that had been successfully used in the Mexican War and in Europe. McClellan was particularly enamored of Napoleonic tactics, as the lances had been successfully used in the Napoleonic wars.

While many of the Union's new volunteer cavalry regiments went into service in the summer of 1861, the Lancers were only being formed in the fall of that year. Consequently, in November 1861, McClellan sent a note to Rush: "How would you like to organize your regiment as lancers?" Rush responded immediately, "Your wishes would be my choice. The material of my regiment is fully equal to the lance. I would consider the selection an honor."[10] Because there were no other weapons available to the men of the 6th Pennsylvania, Rush had little choice but to agree to McClellan's request.

Each man received a nine-foot-long wooden lance tipped with an eleven-inch-long steel blade. The lances, copies of an Austrian pattern, each weighed about eight pounds and were topped by a scarlet pennant, which became a handy target for Confederate sharpshooters. They proved cumbersome and impractical in the wooded terrain of the eastern seaboard; Cpl. Joseph Blaschek of Company M later recalled that the lances were "a decided nuisance in a wooded country." Another trooper wrote, "the officers like it, but the men do not, and the officers wouldn't if they had to use [it]. . . ." The lances also made the men of the regiment something of a laughingstock in the army. Maj. Alexander Biddle of the 121st Pennsylvania

Volunteer Infantry wrote home to his wife, a first cousin of Richard Rush, "I was told today that their little pennants are called 'hospital flags' derisively."[11] Certainly, the lances set the men of the regiment apart, but they proudly wore the name Rush's Lancers.

McClellan believed that it would take two years to adequately train volunteer cavalry, and few in 1861 believed that the war would last that long. Consequently, there was a major debate among the high echelons of the Federal command about how to properly use and arm the many volunteer cavalry regiments raised in the summer of 1861. Biased against volunteer cavalry, McClellan believed in late 1861, "For all present duty of cavalry in the upper Potomac volunteers will suffice as they will have *nothing to do but carry messages & act as videttes*" (emphasis added). A week later, McClellan requested that no more volunteer cavalry regiments be raised throughout the North, since their role was unclear, and there were questions about the army's ability to mount and arm the new recruits.[12] Thus, the role of Rush's Lancers remained undefined in the fall of 1861.

One of Rush's Lancers was Thomas W. Smith of Philadelphia. When he enlisted for a three-year term on October 10, 1861, Smith was twenty-three years old. Prior to enlisting, the young bachelor resided with his parents, Joseph R. and Cathy Smith, in their home in the busy and bustling part of Philadelphia, at the intersection of Twelfth and Market Streets. His mother was evidently in poor health much of the time, and little is known about his father. The 1860 census records indicate that Joseph R. Smith, who listed his occupation as "Gentleman," was fifty years old and owned his home, which was worth sixty-five hundred dollars, a princely sum in the antebellum period. Tom had two brothers: Joseph W., an eighteen-year-old salesman, and Benjamin, known as Bennie, age nine. He also had two sisters: Susan, a twenty-year-old sales clerk, and Jane, also known as Jennie, age thirteen.[13]

Tom joined the cavalry, and his brother Joe served in the Pennsylvania Emergency Militia during the public hysteria accompanying the September 1862 Confederate invasion of Maryland. An upholsterer by trade, young Smith was tall for a cavalryman at five feet, nine inches and weighed about 145 pounds.[14] While not of the upper class and not college educated, he nevertheless possessed a keen if untrained mind and acute powers of observation. These traits shone through time and again in the letters he wrote home.

In early October 1861, Smith walked the four blocks down Market Street to Colonel Rush's recruiting office, located at 833 Market Street, and enlisted in Company I of the Lancers. Raised in both Philadelphia and Chester County, Pennsylvania, Company I consisted of approximately one hundred men, commanded by Capt. James Starr, another Philadelphian. Most of the company mustered into the service during October, and its men immediately set about mastering the art of war. Smith was popular enough with his comrades in the company that he was elected corporal almost immediately. As corporal, he was responsible for teaching other new recruits their duties, enforcing discipline, and assisting the company sergeants in the performance of their duties.[15]

The men established Camp Meigs, a training camp in the northeast part of Philadelphia, wherein they began learning to be soldiers. Shortly after Smith's enlistment, the unit received its regimental flag in a stirring patriotic ceremony featuring a speech by Colonel Rush. On December 4, a parade was held through the streets of Philadelphia. The regimental historian, Chaplain Samuel L. Gracey, recorded: "This was one of the finest cavalry displays ever witnessed in [Philadelphia], and the only time that a regiment of Lancers was ever seen on its streets. The lance being new and highly burnished; the scarlet pennon bright and attractive; the new uniform, and the tidy appearance of men and horses, all combined to render it a brilliant and imposing pageant."[16]

After the review, Governor Curtin made a long and patriotic speech, stating, "You go to vindicate the history of the past, and to make that of the present." Ready for action or not, on October 28, 1861, Secretary of War Simon Cameron had ordered the Lancers to come to Washington and report to McClellan for orders.[17] Although Rush was ordered to "bring . . . [his] regiment with its organization . . . to Washington without delay," it took more than a month for the command to march. They traveled by train to Meridian Hill in Washington, D.C., where they established Camp Barclay, named for their patron.

By December 16, the entire regiment had reached Washington and set about drilling in earnest. The young soldiers were also homesick. Lt. Theodore Sage of Company B wrote home on December 24: "All the boys in the tent are setting around wishing that they could be in Philadelphia for a few hours but wishing will not do much."[18] It was clear that political pressures would bring a spring campaign for the newly christened Army of the Potomac, and the new cavalrymen had to be ready for the ardors of the field. Smith's first surviving letter home was written early in 1862; little is known of his early days of service other than that he was present for duty with his company in both Philadelphia and Washington,[19] and there the story begins.

– CHAPTER ONE –

"We Drill from Morning to Night Now"

———

Early 1862—
Learning to Be a Soldier

Tom Smith spent the first portion of 1862 learning to be a soldier and becoming accustomed to life in the army. It was a difficult transition for someone who had never before lived away from home. Of course, Smith was not alone—nearly all of the volunteer soldiers in both armies were going through the same changes. His letters during the first months of 1862 reflect the difficulty he endured while learning his new trade as well as offer great insight into the day-to-day life of a cavalry trooper in the early days of the Civil War.

Much of the allure of soldiering had worn off by the first month of 1862. Instead, the untried Lancers settled into a boring routine of waiting for the weather to break and finding ways to relieve the tedium.

Camp Barclay
Jan 7/62

Dear Sister

I received yours of the 11th inst. and was very happy as I always am and always will be to hear from home. Our grubb is getting somewhat better as we have had fresh Beef twice in the last 7 Days, and we have fresh Bread 2 Days out of 5.

Tell mother that that dollar was a God send to me and was very thankfully Received as I was dead Broke and had nary Red to Rest my Eyes on. We made a parade through Washington on new years day and were to be Reviewed By Gen McClellan and staff. But were disappointed on account of the illness of the Gen.[1]

We have had very rough weather for the last week. There is about 4 inches of snow on the ground now and you may believe our horses suffer very much, we have Burried 6 Horses out of our company since we have been here. I must now close as I have not time to scribble any more and I dont believe you can Read what I have done. I will not write any more untill after Pay day and then I will send mother some money.[2] But I cannot send as much as I will buy myself a pair of Gloves and Boots to keep my feet warm. I dont care how much they cost. I hope that this will find you well as I am. Write soon and give my love to all the family.

Yours affectionately,
Tom

———

Camp Barclay
Jan 15th/62

Dear Joe

When I wrote my last letter, I thought I would not write any more untill we where paid off, which I thought would be last week. But having received your letter of the 13th and having nothing else to do on account of the weather, I thought I would write a few lines to you just for the sake of passing away time, which hangs rather heavy at pressent. We have had nothing but rain and snow since the 7th inst., and you may judge that it is not very plessant setting in our tents for over a week with nothing to do but eat and sleep. This morning when we awoke it was snowing and hailing which soon turned to a cold and heavy Rain, and as I write I can see our horses tied in front of our Tents covered with Ice, and Icesickles hanging to them a half yard long. Our tents began to leak with so much Ice and Snow on them all the time, but with our India Rubber coats and a hot fire we manage to keep ourselves very comfortable.

I have received several papers from you which are always very acceptable.

Our regiment has been detailed to take charge of Washington City to act as a patrol and two Companys went to the City this morning, they will stay two weeks, and when they come back two more will go and so on untill we will all get a chance.[3]

I wrote a letter to Carter last week he has not answered it yet, and I suppose he did not get it as I did not know where to direct it. If you see him tell him that I wrote.

I have no more to say at pressent give my Love to all the family, write soon.

Yours affectionately,
Tom

P.S. Whiskey I have smelt Twice since I have been here but nary a taste.

Tom

Life in Camp Barclay was not terribly interesting. With the wretched weather, there were few opportunities for the men to engage in outdoor activity, so they spent much of their time just trying to stay warm and dry. As one member of the regiment wrote home, "When the weather was fair our officers let no time pass by unemployed, but for the past two weeks, in consequence of the inclemency of the weather, the drill has been almost entirely dispensed with. It has been exceedingly disagreeable in camp since the rain set in. The mud has been ankle deep, indeed, in some places knee deep; still we have managed to keep our tents dry and warm." Also on January 15, Capt. Robert Milligan of Company F of the Lancers wrote, "Here we still are lying idle on Meridian Hill, pining for active service."[4] Obviously, boredom affected the regiment's officers, too.

Camp Barclay
Jan 26th/62

Dear Mother

I take this opportunity of writing a few lines to you. I received a letter from Conny and I was surprised to see that she wrote such a good letter. I had to laugh about Ben[5] and his Rabits. Tell him to take good care of them that I want to see them when I come home.

The weather still continues bad. We have not had a clear day for the last 18 days and I am Realy Surprised that there is not more Sickness in our camp that what there is.

Another [of] the boys in our camp have been receiving boxes from home and now as I want some Tobacco I think I will get you to send me one.

I want 3¹/₂ lbs of Rough and Ready Tobacco. Tell Joe to get it at Fred Zimmerman's in Market St. above Eleventh and tell him that it is for me and to save him good moist tobacco. I want 25 sheats of Letter Paper and 25 Envelopes. Get them at Magees in Chestnit St above 3ʳᵈ. Get them with Col Rush's Likeness on. If you have anything else in the way of Edibles to send you make up a Box and send it by Addams Express. I will get it the day after sent. So you need not be afraid of anything spoiling.

We got paid off yesterday and Enclosed I will send you Ten Dollars $10.00 which is all that I can spare this time as I had to buy a pair of Boots and a pair of gloves. Hoping that this may find you all as I am.

I remain your,
Affectionate son,
Tom

P.S. Please send me an account of what those articles cost which you send. I wish you would send me a Receipt how to make Buckwheat Cakes and how much yeast to put in and what kind of yeast cakes to get. Please answer Immediately and let me know wheather you Received this safely.

Tom

Tom evidently missed the taste of whiskey. Army policy prohibited the men from having liquor, except for medicinal purposes, so it was often in demand in the camps. As we shall see in the next letter, Tom, like many of his fellow soldiers, was not above using subterfuge to get a good bottle of whiskey. Judging from the end of the letter, we can assume that his parents would not have approved of Joe's sending whiskey to Tom.

Camp Barclay
Jan 26th/62

Dear Brother

I sent mother a letter with some money $10.00 in it and I want her to send me a Box with some Tobacco &c. I sent Directions where to get it and I want you to get it for me. Enclosed I send you $1.00 and I want you to send me a quart of good Whiskey if you see Bill Turner you can get him to get it for me if not you can get some of your friends to get it who are a good judge. You can tell the folks that I want it for medical purposes. Please answer and let me know if you Received this safely.

Your brother,
Tom

Washington, D.C., was a land of opportunity for profiteers during the early phases of the Civil War. Lincoln's first secretary of war, Pennsylvanian Simon Cameron, would prove to be one of the most corrupt politicians in the country. It was often said of Cameron's Washington, "You can sell anything to the government at almost any price you've got the guts to ask."[6] Cameron's greed created an atmosphere where it was easy for opportunistic shopkeepers to take advantage of the influx of soldiers into the city and to capitalize on their naivete. It was common for corrupt merchants to sell both the government and the soldiers serving it shoddy goods. Tom Smith was a bit more worldly than many of his fellow soldiers, and he refused to be taken advantage of.

Camp Barclay
Feb 1st/62

Dear Brother

I received your Letter of Jan 26th and I was very Agreeably surprised to find that you are coming on so well with your writing. Your letter was verry plain and I could read every word of it at the first glance. Yesterday I got Leave of Absence from camp. I went to Washington City and of all the Mud Holes that I have been in I think that Washington will take the Premium. The Store Keeppers and People in general are nothing but a set of Thieves and sharpers and their main object is to cheat the soldiers out of their money. I went into a Barber Shop and got Shaved Hair Cut and Shampooed after it was done I asked how much I owed and what do you think he said only $1.25. Of course I paid it in a horn, I gave him 50 cents and told him to go to the Devil.

Sam Boyer,[7] that is one of my mess mates, was with me and from the Barber Shop we went to a Boot Store. Sam picked out a pair of boots and they wanted $10.00 for them. Sam wanted them for $8.00 and while he was bargaining for them I stood at the stove with the boots in my hands, they got a little warm and one of the soles fell off. I walked over to Sam and handed him the Boots. He took hold of them twisted both heels, threw them down and walked out of the Store with the curses of the store keeper after us.

The Public Buildings in Washington are very fine but take them away and it is the meanest City in all Creation. I arrived at Camp about 6 o'clock in the Evening Perfectly disgusted with Washington. There was a fine Drisley Rain falling all the time that I was there and last night it snowed and hailed all night and today it was Pouring Rain. That's the way the weather has been for the last month and I don't believe it will ever be any better.

The place of the Orderly Sergeant was filled by a young man named Morrow[8] from Company C. He was appointed by the Colonel. Tell Sue that I Received her letter of Jan 28th and that I was Realy Horrified at her great trouble, blocked up in Snow 15 squares from home no umbrella why it was terrible to think of. It made my Hair stand on end considering to that the snow was not so deep but what the cars could still run yet why how did she get home or maybe she is not home yet. Tell her to write soon and ease my mind. I hope she did not get her feet wet mine have not been dry since I have been here and I have got so accustomed to it that when I put on a dry Pair of stockings it makes me feel very disagreeable.

My health still continues good except a Bad Cold and there is not a man in the Regiment that is clear of that. There was a young man out of our company died yesterday morning. His name was Arnold he was from Chester County. He died with the typhoid fever.[9] His body was sent home. Good bye. Give my love to all the familey. Write soon again.

Tom

The tedium of camp life continued unabated. The miserable winter weather still had not broken, the Army of the Potomac had not broken its winter camp, and life for the men of the 6th Pennsylvania consisted of drilling, when the weather permitted, and guard duty. A member of the regiment wrote on February 8, "Nothing but rain, rain, rain, snow, snow, mud, mud, mud."[10] It was not a terribly interesting stint of duty for the Lancers.

Camp Barclay
Feb 14th/62

Dear Brother:

I received your letter the other day. I was busy at the time and I just opened it and put it in my Pocket and that was the last I seen of it, so if I don't answer it correctly you must excuse me. You must tell mother to excuse me for not writing sooner. The weather has been very fine for the past few Days and we have got to Drilling again and I tell you it keeps us buisy to keep our things in order for the mud is about a foot deep.

Our Colonel is now absent from camp, he is in Philadelphia to attend the Funeral of his Brother J. Murry Rush. Our Captain also has just returned from a visit home perhaps you have seen him.[11]

That Box came to hand in good time and in good order, tell Mother that it was very Tastefully got up and very thankfully received. I did Receive that dollar in Bennies letter.

Dear Joe today I am on Guard this morning. It was clear and I thought we would have a fine day on Guard for once but now it is Raining and Hailing like Thunder.[12] I have not had a fine day on Guard ever since I first went to camp, and I begin to think that I will never have one.

Last week the non coms of the Regiment presented Col. Rush with a sword. We had it made in Philadelphia and it was a very handsome affair. The gripe was made of sollid silver bound round with Gold. It took 27 half dollars to make it the Guard, the rings, and Bands were Gold. The Scabbard was made of Blued steel and Gold mountings. It cost One Hundred and Fifty Dollars $150.00 and was made by our Orderly Sergeant's Father.[13]

My health still continues good, I was weighed the other day and weighed 146 lbs, which is about the same weight as I was when I was at Home. No more now at present. Hoping that you all are well, I remain,

Your affectionate Brother,
Tom

P.S. Give my Love to all the Family and all inquiring Friends. I am verry sorry to hear of Turners misfortune. Tell him that he Promised me that after he got out of the seller he would quit drinking. I have not felt so downharted since I left Home as I did when I heard of his misfortune.

The following was an addendum to Smith's letter of February 14.

Feb 15th/62

Dear Joe:

I Sealed and directed this Letter yesterday and put in the charge of our quartermaster sergent[14] and this afternoon it was handed to me without any envelope. I have traced it up to four different men in our company and the last one said he did not know the Person that handed it to him. There has been several letters missed lately and it is supposed that some person in our company steals them. We are going to set a trap for him and God help the Thief if he is caught for we wont have any mersy on him.

Tom

No evidence exists that either Smith or his friends ever solved the mystery of who was stealing the company's mail. In the meantime, the war continued in a holding pattern. Since the late fall campaigning at Big Bethel, the Army of the Potomac had done little but drill and prepare for a spring campaign, and its men eagerly anticipated taking the field again.

The Lancers were also excited about the prospect of getting away from the stagnation of Camp Barclay. Capt. Robert Milligan wrote, "We are more ignorant of what is going on immediately round you in quiet, stupid Wilmington [Delaware]."[15] Finally, rumors of an impending movement reached Camp Barclay, welcome news to the ears of the Lancers. Smith's next letter was intended to be secret, so that only his brother Joe knew that the regiment had been ordered to march. However, no record of these orders exists, and it does not appear that the Lancers ever actually marched in obedience to those orders, indicating that this was an unsubstantiated rumor.

Joseph W. Smith
Private
Feb 15th/62

Dear Joe:

We are under marching orders this morning. The Companys were called out by their Captains. Our Captain told us to get everything in order that there was to be a great moove on the other side of the River [16] and that we would be with it. He said that there would be 60 of the best Men picked out of each Company that we might go in an hour or that we might not go for three weeks. We are to take no tents nor nothing but one Blanket and our Over Coats. He said we might come back and if not that our tents and Property would be sent on to us. I give you the facts as I know them. Dont let any of the Family know this as it will only give them trouble. But I think we will see a Battle before Long. Give my best wishes to all my Friends. Let me know if you have seen Carter lately. I will try and get time to write to him soon.

Tom

P.S. We Drill from morning to night now.

On February 19, 1862, the men received new scarlet pennants for the ends of their lances, a gift from the women of Philadelphia.[17] Suitably out-fitted, the men set out to master their weapons.

Camp Barclay
Feb 28th/62

Dear Brother

I received your Letter some time since, and you must excuse me for not answering it sooner as I have been so buisy that I can't get time to write any more. Tell Jane that I tried to bake Buckwheat Cakes once but Failed, every thing went well until I went to Bake them. I had nothing but a thin Frying Pan and it burnt them all up so I got mad and throwed the batter away. So much for Buckwheat Cakes.

We have not been attached to any Brigade yet, Camp Casey is about one mile from our camp.[18]

All the drill that we have had in the Lance Exercise is Charge Lance and Carry Lance. The Saber and Pistol exercise we are very good on. We have orders not to wear our Dress Hats any more and some of the Companeys have given them up, we are to get new ones but what kind I cannot say.

Joe you need not send any more papers as we can get all the Papers here now, but I wish you would send me the Sunday Transcript.[19]

Dear Joe look out for newes. From all that I can hear and see I think there will be a Grand Forward Movement of the Grand Army of the Potomac and I hope to God that it will not be another Bull Run affair.

Lieutenant Jackson of our company has been detached from our Regiment to serve on General Kees staff on the other side of the River.[20] He left us yesterday and we were all verry sorry to part with him.

No more at present. Give my Love to all the Family. Hoping that you are all well, I remain,

Your affectionate Brother,
Tom

P.S. The whiskey came all Safe and it was verry good. I would give 25 cts for a good Glass now as it is as cold as the Devel. Did you get that Letter that I sent for Bill. If so let me know as soon as possible.

On March 10, the Lancers finally got orders to march. The bulk of the Army of the Potomac was camped near the old Bull Run battlefield at Manassas, Virginia. Chaplain Gracey wrote, "The regiment presented a fine appearance as, with colors flying, and band playing, they passed through the city, and started out for active service. The men were in buoyant spirits as they bid farewell to winter quarters, and took the field for earnest work."[21] The Lancers marched across the Chain Bridge and about ten miles into Virginia, where they joined the Fourth Corps of Gen. Erasmus D. Keyes.

Camp Barclay
midnight, March 16/62

Dear Brother

Being on Guard tonight and having no accomidations to sleep, I thought I would try and write a few lines to you for the sake of keeping awake. When I wrote to you last we were laying on Cannon Farm Prospect Hill, Virginia awaiting orders to march on. We laid there untill Friday morning at 4 o'clock. The Bugle sounded saddle up and immediately everything was in a bustle. We were packed and saddled by 5 o'clock and at 6 we were ordered to mount and we with the whole Division took up our line of march on the Back track to Chain Bridge where we were to wait for further Orders. We waited there untill nightfall and no orders came. It then began to rain and we were ordered to unpack our Horses and Picket them in the woods and make ourselves as comfortable as possible. We staid there untill Saturday night at 7 o'clock when General Keys gave orders that if we wished we could go to camp and wait there for further orders. Our bugle blown saddle up and our Boys were soon in their way to Camp which they Reached about 11 o'clock. Our quartermaster sergent was absent and I was detailed to take his place. I had to see our Company stores be all loaded before I could Leave, so it was 2 o'clock before I got to camp. It rained like the Devel and I was wet through. My blankets extra clothing and every thing I had was soaked. I do not think we stay here long as we were told this morning to get our Blankets and Clothing dry and keep our saddles packed. I do not know where we are going to but I suppose the Reason we were sent back was because the Rebbels are retreating before us but I suppose we are wanted in some other place. There is a Rumer that we are going to Roanoke Island.

I have not seen a paper for over a week. When you write let me know how we stand with the Sesesh and what movements our armey had made.

I received a letter from Father today and I was Glad to hear that he and Mother and the rest of the Family are well. By the way if you have got a dollar to lend let me have it as soon as possible if not sooner as I am out of Tobacco and dead Broke.

I don't know weather you can Read this or not, but a wood fire in the open air is not the best light to write by. One minute it is too hot the next too cold then no light and then the smoke in your Eyes. It is verry near 4 o'clock when I must post my relief so I must close. Give my love to all the family and all inquiring Friends.

Your affectionate brother,
Tom

P.S. Direct your letters to Washington or Elsewhere and I will get it if we do moove.

The Lancers did not enjoy their first foray into the field. Their bivouac was cold, wet, and miserable from the heavy rains. When they marched back to Camp Barclay, they "were rejoiced to find tents still standing, and dry shelter awaiting them. This being our first trip to 'Dixie,' was a very rough introduction to field service, and has been remembered in the regiment as the Prospect Hill 'Mud March.'"[22] Soon, the Lancers were back to the familiar and monotonous routine of camp life.

Camp Barclay
March 20th/62

Dear Brother

I received your letter of the 18th Inst. and also the two dollar bill which Mother sent. I do not believe we will be paid for some time yet as they have not paid any of the Troops about here yet and there is talk of letting it run on for 4 months. But I hope not as our Boys are sadley in need of their money.

We are hourly expecting marching orders. Our Colonel told us yesterday that when we march from here again it will be by water, he didnt say where we are going to, but I think it will up the Rappahanock River.

I received the Sunday Transcript that you sent me which is the first paper I have seen for at least 10 Days. I am Glad to hear that you are all well at home. Give my Love to all the Family and write soon again.

Brother Tom

P.S. Where is Turner

I have just received Tuesdays Press. I suppose that you sent it.

Rumors of the impending movement of the entire Army of the Potomac to the Virginia Peninsula for a grand assault on Richmond reached the camp of the Lancers.

Camp Barclay
March 27th/62

Dear Mother

I take this opportunity of writing a few lines to you. We were paid off yesterday. I had intended when paid to send you more money than what I do but our Captain told me that the Regiment was shown a great favour by being paid off the first and he told me that I had better keep as much money as I could as were going to a Place where we would want it and that he thought we would not be paid again for at least 6 months. We are all Ready to March and expecting orders every moment.

I went to Washington yesterday after we were paid off and while there I met Captain Starr. He told me to get specia for my tresury notes for in the Country where we were going to they were worth no more than so much News Paper.[23] I had to go to a Broker and it cost me 4 percent for change. By the way I may as well tell you here that I have over drawn my years allowance for clothing to the amount of $2.63 cts. Two dollars and sixty three cents which was taken out of my pay this time. We are allowed Clothing to the amount of $49.57 per year and at that price they charged us our first outfit amounted to $45.00.

Enclosed I send you $10.00. Write soon as you get this and if we are not here your letter will follow us. I must now close as our mail is Ready.

Yours affectionately,
Tom

On March 30, the long-awaited orders to march finally arrived. The Lancers saddled up, marched across the Long Bridge, and proceeded to Alexandria, Virginia, where they encamped near Fort Ellsworth, named for the slain Zouave hero, Col. Elmer Ellsworth. They camped there for three days before receiving orders to embark on schooners for the journey down the Chesapeake Bay on April 3. They required seventeen schooners and a number of tugs to convey the entire regiment plus its horses and wagons.[24]

On Board the Schooner
Maryland off Fortress Monroe Apprial 8th/62

Dear Father

I received your letter of March 30th while laying at Alexandria and have not had a chance to answer it sooner. I received those Papers that you sent me. I was a little worried about that letter that I sent to Mother for I began to think that it miscarried.

We left Camp Barclay on Sunday March 30th and marched to Alexandria by way of the Long Bridge. We encamped about one mile Below Alexandria on the Manasses Rail Road. Late in the afternoon it was a verry disagreeable march as it Rained all Day and night.

We layed at Alexandria untill Sunday April 2nd. At noon we saddled up and went to town to ship but we only got four companeys aboard by dark and the Rest of us had to go back and lay on the old ground again until Thursday morning when we went to town again. Our Company was the last one that got aboard. We got the whole Company aboard one schooner the Marryland and at dark we Dropped out into the River and anchored over night. On Friday the 4 inst. we were taken in tow by the Steam Boat Aeriel and made such good head way that by night we had left the whole fleet of about 50 vessels out of sight, when the weather got so rough that the Steam Boat had to leave us and the wind being high and we being loaded top-heavy having 92 horses on Deck we had to anchor over night untill the storm was over. The next morning Satturday we got under way and the Aeriel soon came up and took us in tow and we made good time untill 4 o'clock. In the afternoon we were out of sight of land there was a Regular Storm sprung up. Our tow lines broke and we went scudding before the wind at a great rate. We soon lost sight of the Steam Boat so we made for the Virginia shore and we anchored off the Rappahanock about 9 o'clock at night. At 4 o'clock in the morning Sunday the wind died off and we got under sail and anchored off Fortress Monroe[25] at dark. We were to land here but it seems there had been a Battle fought at Yorktown on the York River and our forces have got the worst of it and want Reinforcements, there was a steamer sent up the Bay to stopp all transports of troops, and tell them to turn in at York River, but they missed our Company and that accounts for us being the only Company our of the Regiment that arrived here. The weather has been so rough that we could not go back yet, and today it is Raining very hard and the wind is very high. As soon as it clears off we will go back to York River and land, and for my part I don't care how soon for we have had nothing but hard crackers and water ever since we came aboard.

The Monitor is laying about one hundred yards from us and curious looking affair she is, all that is to be seen of her is a Round Iron Tub and a sentinel walking on top of it.[26]

Our Regiment has been Brigaded with 4th and 5th U.S. Regular Cavalry. I must close as the Captain is going ashore and I want to send this. My love to all.

Yours affectionately,
Tom

As Smith pointed out to his father, the Lancers were to join the Army of the Potomac's Cavalry Reserve, commanded by Brig. Gen. Philip St. George Cooke, the senior cavalry officer in the U.S. Army. Cooke, the father-in-law of Confederate cavalry chief J. E. B. Stuart, was considered the father of the U.S. Cavalry. By the outbreak of the war, Cooke had already served in the U.S. Army for thirty-four years. Despite his great reputation as a cavalryman, Cooke's time probably had come and gone. Capt. Emlen N. Carpenter of Company G of the 6th Pennsylvania astutely observed, "Gen. Cooke is an old man & has not the vim necessary to maneuver against [Stuart]."27

Cooke's Cavalry Reserve consisted of two brigades. The First Brigade, commanded by Brig. Gen. William H. Emory, consisted of the Fifth and Sixth U.S. Cavalry regiments and the Lancers. The Fifth and Sixth U.S. were part of the U.S. Army's Regular mounted force, although the Sixth U.S. was a new regiment, formed during the summer of 1861. Emory was a fifty-two-year-old West Pointer who had been in the Regular Army for nearly thirty years by the outbreak of the Civil War. A cavalryman from Massachusetts noted that Emory was "a fine specimen of the old United States army officer." A hero of the Mexican War, he was commanding cavalry for the first time. Profane and eccentric, he was known as "Old Brick Top" for the color of his hair. Emory was unpopular with the men who served under him. One officer wrote home, "The General is grossly neglectful of us."28

The formation of the Cavalry Reserve represented the first time that the army had formed cohesive brigades of cavalry, and it was fortunate that the Lancers were grouped with the army's professional horse soldiers. Because McClellan generally did not trust the volunteer cavalry regiments, the Regular cavalry regiments were to provide the bulk of the army's traditional cavalry roles, such as scouting, picketing, and screening the advance of the army.

> Hampton Virginia
> April 8th 1862

Dear Sister

I wrote a Letter to Father a few Days ago while laying aboard the Schooner Maryland, at that time we expected to be sent to York Town whare Eight

Companeys of our Regiment had gone Before us, but they had more
Cavalry than they wanted so they had orders to come back and land at
Fortress Monroe. On the 9th Inst. I and E Companeys landed at 9 o'clock in
the morning and we proceded to Hampton (or rather the ruins of
Hampton) and there Encamped to await the arrival of the Ballance of our
Regiment. The last two Companeys F and G arrived at the Fortress this
Evening, and will be in camp tomorrow morning. Company G had a Rough
time of it, they were without Feed for men or horses for 48 hours. I do not
think we will stay here long, for as soon as the Regiment get together we
will moove forward.

From all apperineces [appearances] Hampton has been a verry fine
place, and I should judge had about 2000 inhabitants. There was Eight
Churches in the place. But when the Rebels Retreated they applied the
Torch to Every thing not only in the Town but of all the houses as far as we
can see there is but three standing.[29] Even the corner stones of the
Churches have been dug up, and Graves and vaults have been torn open by
our Troops for plunder I suppose. Such is war.

This morning the Merrimac[30] made her appearance, in the James River
with seven Gun Boats in Company with her, and as soon as it was known,
Every Body made for the shore to see the Fun. I secured a good position
on the top of a mast of one of the schooners laying at the wharf. The
Merrimac was laying off Sewels Point about 4 mile from where I was. All
our shipping made for the Fortress, the shores were Black with men and
the Rigging of the Shipping were crowded. The Rebel Fleet captured 3 old
Schooners that were unable to get out of her way in time. Our Little Cheese
Box—the Monitor, and the Stevens Battery were under steam waiting for
her to come down the River, but she would not come within Range of their
guns. In the middle of the Afternoon the Stevens Battery ran up opposite to
Hampton and Fired several shotts at the Merrimac to try and draw her out
but she would not take the bait. So the Stevens Battery ran back to the
Fortress again. They were about two miles distant when they exchanged
shotts and one of our shotts struck the M[errimack] on the side but as near
as I could see done no dammage. I expect they will have some fun
tomorrow and I shall try and get down to see it.

I hear that we have whipped the Rebbels again in Tennessee[31] and this
morning there is a Report that we have taken York Town.[32] I begin to fear
that we will have the Rebbles conquered before our Regiment sees service.

But I hope not as I would like to be in one Battle to see what our Lances are good for before the war is over.

Father tells me that your health is . . . [the remainder of this letter is missing]

While Tom Smith witnessed history in the making at Hampton Roads, the Lancers prepared to make their first foray into battle. Soon they would see combat as McClellan's giant army advanced up the Virginia Peninsula toward Richmond, the Confederate capital. There, they would face the enemy for the first time.

CHAPTER TWO

"We Have Had Quite Stirring Times about Here"

Thomas Smith in
McClellan's Peninsula Campaign

MCCLELLAN BELIEVED THAT HE could capture the Confederate capital by assaulting it from the east. Two corps of his army were left behind, but remaining troops participated in this movement. McClellan moved west up the Peninsula from his base of operations at Fortress Monroe. The Army of the Potomac launched its movement on Richmond from the finger of land protruding into the Chesapeake Bay created by the convergence of the James and York Rivers. His army of more than ten thousand men moved slowly, as McClellan believed that his force was outnumbered by the Confederates, who actually had less than half his available manpower.

McClellan's delay in front of the Revolutionary War battlefield at Yorktown cost his advance two full weeks, giving Confederate general Joseph E. Johnston time to rally his forces in front of Richmond and costing McClellan's army the opportunity to capture the Southern capital easily. The Federal advance was further slowed in front of Williamsburg by a small force of Rebel infantry. Finally, McClellan shook himself free of the Confederates and marched on Richmond. The Lancers were about to taste combat for the first time.

Tom Smith continued his steady correspondence home. Most of his letters were still to his brother Joe, but he also wrote to his sister Susan and his parents. His letters reflect a young soldier's excitement and trepidation at seeing action for the first time. They also demonstrate his characteristic candor and a keen sense of observation, as the following letter shows.

[undated]

Dear Joe

Since I wrote my last Letter Home I have received three—two from you and one from Mother on last Munday. A week ago we left Hampton as we thought for York Town but after marching 3 miles we Halted and here we are yet. I think that Sister Sue will have her wish grattified which she expressed in her last letter about our Lances. I dont think that we will ever get a chance to try them. Last Friday the Regiment was inspected by General Stoneman,[1] and staff and when we came to the Inspection of armes, (By the way, at the command Inspection Armes the lance is inspected first, then the saber, then the pistols). He the General said Raise them Damn poles I don't want to see them. Colonel Rush has orders to turn the lances in by the 10th of May, or else Report the Regiment to Governor Curtin in Harrisburgh.

Now last Friday morning at 10 o'clock we went out about 5 miles from Camp to Pasture our Horses on the Banks of the James River. We had to go through woods and swamps and ditches and we had not been there long before the Colonel sent word for us to come Back to Camp Immediately that we were to be inspected at one o'clock. We galloped all the way back to camp and got there at 15 minutes after 12 o'clock with the men and horses covered with mud. The General[2] found falt with the condition of our Horses, and in the evening Rush called the Regiment out and gave us orders to clean our horses Three Hours every day one and a half Hours before Breakfast and the same after Drill in the afternoon. Ever since the Inspection Rush has Played the Tyrent to Perfection. One day last week while the Regiment was on Drill he sent a guard around and found 10 men off Drill most of them were washing. He called a drum head court martial, and had them fined to the amount of $61 sixty one dollars to be taken out of their Pay. It is customary when a Field Officer approaches the Guard House to turn out the Guard and Present Armes. Last Sunday the Colonel went there and it so Happened that there was a verry ignorant man on number one post whose duty it is to notify the Guard by calling out Field Officers, Turn out the Guard, which he neglected to do. Rush got into one Hell of a Pashion, put the man in the Guard House and not satisfyed with this fell to cursing all the men who were there. His first words were, you are a God Damn pretty number one you Damn Sons of Bitches you and so he went on cursing the whole Regiment for about 10 minutes all for the mistake of one man. Ever since we have been in service our officers (the majority of whom are Beardless Boys and Belong to the Class generally known in Philadelphia as the Ginger Bread Aristocracy[3]) have been trying to get the Regiment accepted as Regulars, and have Tyronised over the men and Ground them down more than any Regulars which it has been my luck to meet with yet. Why Regulars are freemen besides us we have always got a heavy Guard on. The men come on Guard Every 3 and 4 days and there are guards all around the camp. We cant get 50 yards away from our Tents, while in other Regiments when the men are off-duty they can go where they pleese, they can go and visit other camps and meet with some of their friends. While here we cannot go out and lately they will not even let other soldiers come in and see a friend. I think I told you that we had been Bregaded with the 4th and 5th Regulars. Well we have been changed again, we are now bregaded with the 8th Penna.[4] The Colonel of the Regulars is our Brigadeer General and the Colonel of the 8th is the Commanding officer of the bregade[5] and this is what galls Rush so much.

And now for a few words about Company I. When we left Philadelphia we had the name of having the best set of non coms of any company in the Regiment. And we had, but now we have the worst. Corporal Jove[6] and Sergent Malsberger[7] have been Reduced to the ranks and they were as good if not the best non coms we had. Sergent Malsperger was Reduced because he went to the Captain[8] and asked to the Transferred to the Regulars. According to the late bill passed by Congress the Captain gave his consent but a few days after the men got to hear of it and 16 of them went and wanted to be transferred also and what do you suppose Captain Starr done? Why he sent the men all to the guard house kept them there for two days and Reduced Malsperger to the Ranks. Our non coms now are Orderly sergent Abe Price[9] verry good.

Quartermaster Sergent Price Kepner[10] a snot of a boy who thinks his duty is to curse and sware at the men call them Sons of Bitches and send two men to the Guard House everey week.

1st Duty Sergent Richard Finn[11] a sleeppy poke who has nothing to say to the men and who has got two much influence at home to be reduced to the Ranks.

2nd Sergent Lawrence Pennington[12] verry good.

3rd Sergent Michel Towers[13] a perfect Gentelman who is loved by the whole company. He knowes his duty and performs it.

4th Sergent Edward McGratton[14] a thing who in Private Life was a Hod Carrier and can neither read nor write. He was promoted because he knows how to dommineer over the men. He never tells a man to do anything without an oath.

2nd Corp Sam Wright.[15]

3rd Corp James Boon[16] a Good Fellow.

4th Corp Sam Wilhour[17] Read McGratton's description.

5th Corp Keller[18] a German and about as much good as a 5th wheel on a waggon.

6th Corp Hamilton[19] McGratton's description.

7th Corp Pat Cardiff.[20]

8th Corp Sam Roberts[21] verry good.

You see we have one Sergent and three Corporals who can neither read nor wright. You may think it queer that I never found falt with the Regiment before but I did not want to let the folks at Home know anything about it. Lately things have come to such a pass that it would be wrong to keep quiet any longer.

I am verry well at Pressent having got rid of that cough that I had. I hope that Sue and the rest of you have got rid of yours too. If Mother gets worse let know Immediately. When I commensed this I intended to coppy it but being on Poliece duty today, I find I will not have time, so you will have to spell it out the best way you can. I must now close as it is now time for the Poliece to get to work.

My best love to all.

Tom

Address all letters as heretofore.

Joe

You had better Read this by yourself first and then you can let the folks know as much as you think proper.

Smith's observations about Richard Rush were not unique. Maj. Alexander Biddle of the 121st Pennsylvania Infantry, married to one of Rush's cousins, observed in a letter home: "Rush is . . . a very unnecessarily mean and severe officer, as regards his treatment of officers in presence of the men. I hear constantly of complaints of treatment which nothing could sanction and I fear he has raised feelings of bitterness which operate up against him."[22]

The Lancers continued to prepare for action, but little happened as they awaited an opportunity to prove themselves in battle. McClellan finally captured Yorktown after the Southern commander, Maj. Gen. John B. Magruder, evacuated the lines on the eve of the planned assault. The Army of the Potomac then moved about thirteen miles farther and took on the Rebel forces at Williamsburg. On May 6, 1862, the regiment received word that disaster had befallen the Federal troops of Gen. Joseph Hooker at Williamsburg the day before, and orders were given for the Lancers to prepare to march. Instead, they spent the night standing to horse in a downpour.[23] This unpleasant duty left the troopers of Company I perplexed, as Smith related to his sister Susan.

Camp Winfield Scott
Near Yorktown
May 7th/62

Dear Sister

I take this opportunity of writing a few lines to you, and I think that this is the first letter I have directed to you since I left Home. The truth is when I write Home I intend my Letters for all the Family, so it don't make any difference who they are directed to.

Last Sunday Morning while our Regiment was out in the field for Inspection the Colonel Received a dispatch, and after Reading it he ordered us to go in, Pack up our duds, and form line ready to march in one hour. We were soon ready and on our way to Yorktown and as we went along we heard that Yorktown was evacuated, and that our Troops were in hot pursuit of the Rebbels. We encamped within a Half mile from the town at 4 o'clock in the afternoon, and Layed there untill Munday Evening at 8 o'clock when we got orders to saddle up and fall in line as soon and as quietly as possible. We were soon in line and after standing there for one hour we were ordered to stand at our horses heads which we did untill 6 o'clock in the morning Tuesday when we got orders to unsaddle and take our horses to the Picket Post. Now what all this was done for I don't know for I don't think there was any danger and if there was they might have told us so instead of keeping us there all night in mud to our knees and a Heavy

Rain and then dismiss us without a word of explanation (it rained from Sunday morning untill Tuesday), but it is verry warm today and if it keeps so it will soon dry this mud off. There is no chance yet to examine the Rebel works about Yorktown as they have Torpedoes[24] buried in the Ground every place, and there has been a great maney of our soldiers killed by them. Yorktown is surrounded by a large fort and trench which extends clear around the town.

The Rebel works here are stronger than anything of the kind that I have seen yet. The Ground is torn up with shell and shott and Every Place you go the ground is strewn with Pieces of Shell and Cannon Balls. There are plenty of Rellicks of the Rebbles here such as 32 lb Balls, exploded shell muskets sabers swords which I would like to send Home, but I have no means of sending them, unless I enclose them in a letter, but if I do that I am afraid they might tare the envelope. Every thing about here is very dear for a Loaf of Bread 5 inches square. We have to pay 15 cts and a man can eat 2 of them at one meal. Tobacco is verry high, yesterday I gave 50 cts for a Piece 10 inches long and $3^1/2$ inches wide and it was the last 50 cts I had. Enclosed I send you a piece of Granite. I broke it off of the Monument Erected on the spot of ground where General Washington stood when he Received the Sword of Lord Cornwallace at the surrender of Yorktown. The Monument is completely demolished.[25] No more at present. Write soon. My love to all the family.

Your affectionate Brother,

Tom

The Lancers stayed around Yorktown until May 9, scouting and picketing, when they finally received orders to join Brig. Gen. William H. Emory's Second Brigade of the Cavalry Reserve. Progress on the eleventh and twelfth was not good, as the roads were blocked by wagon trains, but the Lancers finally joined their brigade on the night of the twelfth. On the thirteenth they marched to Cumberland, where they camped on the farm of a Confederate officer. Finally, on the seventeenth Rush's troopers marched to a place about two miles from White House, where they encamped on a portion of an estate owned by descendants of George Washington.[26] Rumor was that Richmond had been evacuated, and the men were in high spirits, awaiting orders to capture the Rebel capital.[27] While resting near White House, Smith found time to write home.

Barrensville, Virginia
Thursday May 15th/62

Dear Sister

When I wrote my last letter home we were laying in front of Yorktown.
On Friday May 9th about noon we received Orders to join the advance of
General McClellan's Army, we were soon on the Road, but after passing
Yorktown we could get no further on. For we found out that the Road from
Yorktown to Williamsburgh 13 miles was completely blocked up with
Troops and waggon Trains, so we had to go back to our old Camp
Ground and lay there over night.

On Satturday morning Revelree sounded at 2 o'clock and at 3 we were
on the march. We reached Williamsburgh at noon and made a halt one
mile below the town to wait for our waggons to come up, they did not reach
us untill after dark so we had to stay there over night.

Sunday morning we were up again at 2 o'clock and marched 18 miles to
Barnhamsville.[28] We got there at 2 o'clock in the afternoon. We had hardley
got our saddles off of our Horses when Gen. Cook sent word to our
Colonel to send one corporal and one man to his quarters mounted and
fully equipped. Myself and a man from Company K were detailed. We
Reported to Gen. Cook[29] and he told us to go to Mrs. Hagerty's Farm House
about 2 miles distant and guard her Property untill relieved. When we got
there we found that our men had been there and carried off a large quantity
of Corn 3 horses and 2 Head of Cattel.

Mrs. Hagerty who is an Elderly Lady, has 2 sons in the Rebble armey.
Her Daughter who lives with her has a Husband in the army, they have
only been married 2 months. Her Niece a fine young lady of 20 years has
2 Brothers in the army. When the Rebble army left here they took all her
male niggers with them. They have now only 4 gals and nine young
children left, they have a fine Plantation of 500 acres.

When we first came here the Ladies were rather sarcastic and talked a
great deal about the Yankee mudsills and Boasted that their army would
soon drive us off again. But since they have found out our true motives they
have entirely changed. They now treat us like gentlemen and their daily
Prayer is that they may find some means of communication with their
friends in the Rebel armey to get them to throw down their armes and
desert to our lines.

The prevailing opinion here with both Blacks and Whites is that the Blacks are sold off to Cuba to pay the expences of the war and that the white Prisoners are treated in the most cruil and barbarous manner by our soldiers, and I Really believe that two thirds of the Southron army are forsed to take up armes by such lies as these, and if they knew the true state of things they would throw down their armes and end the war tomorrow.

Yorktown is a mean place. There are only about 20 Houses in it.

Williamsburgh is a verry fine place and verry tastefully laid out. As we passed over the Battlefield or the Plain of Williamsburgh as they are called the ground was strewn with armes and clothing of every Description dismounted guns Broken waggons muskets sabers boye knives[30] knapsacks belts &c.

All along the Road from Yorktown where the Reble army Retreated, the Road Bears Indications of the haste in which they left.[31] Gun carriages ammunition waggons and vehicles of every Discription are left standing in the Road, but they always took good care to cut the spokes out of the wheels before abandoning them.

As we passed through Williamsburgh we met the 26th Penna. Vol. Regt. with 500 prisoners in charge and of all the dirty ragget filthy looking men that it was ever my ill fortune to see I think they would take the Prize. Some of them had not enough Rags to cover their nakedness and one Poor Devil had nothing on but a pair of ragget pants and an great ragget Coat that trailed on the Ground it was the Hottest day we have had. They were so dirty that they Really stunk as they passed us.

Every House that we pass they have a large white Flag hanging out. There is not a man to be seen, nothing but women and children. Even of the Slaves they have taken all the men with them. Barrensville[32] is a small village of some Half Dozen Houses a store and a Black Smith shop. It is 18 miles from Williamsburgh, 45 miles from Richmond, and 5 miles from West Point. Our Regiment left here last Munday morning and I guess Gen. Cook has forgotten all about us for we have not heard from him yet, and we dare not Leave here untill we get orders. We have better quarters here than we would have with the Regiment, and better grub to eat. I don't like to be away so long. However it can't be helped so we make the best of it. They want us to sleep in the house but we are afraid to do that for fear of our Horses getting stolen. Besides I have got so used to sleeping on the

Ground, that I am afraid if I was to sleep in a Bed now that I might tumble out and Bump my nose. I sleep in the corn crib and have a string with one end to the stable door and the other end to my foot so that no one can get to the Horses without wakening me.

No more at Pressent. I will send this off the first oppertunity I get. Did Jenny get that Letter I sent, I have not Received an answer yet. Write soon. Give my love to all the Family.

Your affectionate Brother
Tom

While the Lancers still had not seen any combat, they continued to endure miserable living conditions. Smith was not the only member of the regiment to complain. Capt. Robert Milligan wrote home, "I never was so thoroughly uncomfortable in my life. No money no clothes except one change, two towels, no tooth brush. No whiskey, no smoking tobacco, no letter paper, no envelopes, no postage stamps, no pen, and no ink. And no definite prospects of matters getting any better as far as I can see."[33]

On May 18, the Lancers moved to the Richmond and York River Railroad, where they again went into camp, awaiting further orders. On the twentieth they marched six miles and encamped at the Ruffin farm on the Pamunkey River, near Tunstall's Station, Virginia. There they were finally close to the Confederate lines.[34]

19 miles from Richmond
May 20th/62

Dear Sister [Susan]

I stayed at Mrs. Hagertys untill Sunday morning when hearing that Gen Cooks Headquarters were at New Kent Court House, 12 mile distant. I mounted my Horse and started intending to Report to Gen. Cook. Leaving Cary Behind I got onto the rong Road and lost my way in the wood and did not reach New Kent untill 4 o'clock in the afternoon. I found out that Gen. Cook had left there the day before, so I started Back to Barnhamsville where I arrived at dark having rode at least 40 miles. On Munday morning we both left at day Brake (Much against the Ladies will but there was no more danger as our troops had already passed through) to hunt our Regiment and after wandering about the Country all day without finding them we stopped at a place called Baltimore Cross Roads and layed there in the woods over night. This morning (Tuesday) we were off again By Day Break and we found our Regiment at 2 o'clock both our horses and ourselves pretty well worn out. This morning we were verry near the Rebbel lines, having got out as far as our advance Pickets.

When I got to Camp I found Joe's letter, and was verry much supprised to hear that Jenny had not Received my Letter. But I had hardly got through Reading it when the mail arrived and Jenny's Letter with it. Ask Joe how he likes Soldiering.

Tell Jane that I am not yet tired of a soldiers life and that I would not take my discharge if I could get it. As for a furlough it would be impossible to get one at pressent, and I would not take one if I could get it while we are in the face of the enemy.

I am verry sorry to hear that Mother is confined to her bed, and also of your continued Bad Health. If Mother gets worse write and let me know. No more at pressent from your affectionate Brother

Tom

P.S. I Received that two Dollars. Tell Mother not to send any more unless I send her word.

On May 22, the Lancers were sent on a reconnaissance to search for a contingent of Rebel cavalry thought to be in the area. On May 23 they found the enemy and had a brief skirmish. That day, Colonel Rush had an interesting interview with Mrs. Robert E. Lee, whose husband had sent her away from Richmond to escape the advancing Yankee horde, believing that the countryside was safe from the Union army's advance. Rush reported, "The admission of Mrs. Lee that the U.S. Troops were not expected this way, by her family, is so important an item that I deem it proper to report the fact to you at once."[35]

On the twenty-fourth, the Lancers engaged Rebel pickets near Hanover Court House, Virginia. Lt. Theodore Sage noted, "The column returned after being absent about four hours. Our regiment drove in their pickets about two miles when they fell back on their reserve and we returned to camp losing one and no one being injured. There is every probability that there will be some warm work for us in our advance."[36] While on the same reconnaissance, Tom had his first hostile encounter—with a Confederate hog.

Camp Near Old Church Virginia
Sunday May 25th/62

Dear Joe

Last Tuesday when I joined my Regiment, we were laying about one mile
from Turnstall Station, on the Richmond and West Point Rail Road, and a
half mile from the Pamunkey River. We held the extreme Right of the
advance of Gen. McClellan's armey. On the same evening that I arrived
our company went out on Picket 4 miles from Camp. I with 2 men were
stationed on the outer Post, at a place where two Roads meet, and at the
Corner of a large woods. About Midnight I with one of the men, were
standing in the Edge of the Woods on the Bye Road, about 10 yds from the
forks whare I had posted the other man, when he the man on post called out
who comes there. No answer. Halt. Halt. (Phist) which was a signal that it
was comming my way. I heard a Rustling in the leaves and seen a dark
Object comming towards me. I Cocked my Pistol, and waited untill it was
within three Paces of me, when I cried out. Halt or I Fire. The only answer I
Received was a grunt. I couldn't expect anything Else from a Hog. We
returned to camp at day light on Wednesday morning, and at 10 o'clock,
we with the 1st and 5th Regulars, marched about 9 miles. And there we left
our Waggons, and a guard, and each Regiment started in a different
direction to hunt up 2 Regiments of Rebbel Cavalry, which we heard were
out hunting for forage. We took a sircuit of 10 miles and scouted all through
it, but seen nothing of them, though at one time we were only a Half Hour
behind them. We got to our Camp Ground after dark.

On Thursday morning our Regiment marched to Old Church[37] and there
encamped with 2 Regiments of Infantry. The 1st and 5th Regulars stayed
where they were. On Saturday morning we were called up at 2 o'clock, and
ordered to saddel up immediately, without packing our saddles and in
15 minutes we were on the Road at a full Gallop. We went 5 miles and there
waited for our Infantry to come up. They got thare by Day Break when we
started by Squaddrons in different directions. Our Squaddron drove in a
line of the Enemies Pickets, untill we came within sight of their mane
Picket Guard when we Retreated slowly to try and draw them out.
But they would not come. They were encamped in a large piece of woods
and one of them who we captured and also a Negro told us they were
in strong forse, and had Artillery which we had not. So we had to
return to Camp for fear of them cutting off our Retreat. When we drove

in their Pickets we were within three miles of Hanover. Our first Squadron distroyed a Rope ferry, and sunk the ferry Boat and captured three Prisoners.[38]

This Morning we were Reinforsed by 2 Regiments of Infantry, and a Battery of artillery. At 9 o'clock our Division was called out and drawn up in line of Battle, as our Pickets were driven in. But it only Proved to be a squaddron of the Rebble cavelry reconoitering. They fell Back again when they seen our Picket guard so we were dismissed at 11 o'clock and at one our company went out on Picket Duty. I with three men are on post at a Rope ferry, and have orders that if the enemy attempt to cross in the night to cut the Rope sink the Boat and fall back on the mane Guard.[39]

I wish you would send me Floyed's Official Map of the State of Virginia. Price 25 cts. No more at Pressent. Write soon and let me know How Mother is getting. I hope she has got better by this time. Give my love to all the Family.

Your affectionate Brother

Tom

The Lancers had finally contributed to the Union cause by locating the Confederate force at Hanover Court House in one of the first combined force operations of the war, consisting of cavalry, infantry, and artillery. During this advance, Company C of the 6th Pennsylvania made a mounted charge with their lances, scattering the Confederate pickets. The Lancers finally saw combat, although Smith's company was not involved.[40] This reconnaissance also developed the strength of the Confederate force at Hanover Court House. On May 24, Rush reported, "I assume that this morning there was a force at Hanover Court House of not less than 3,000 infantry, six pieces of cannon, and 300 cavalry, four regiments of infantry having arrived day before yesterday. I further think that they are now in sufficient force to move upon us at this point with success, and would suggest at least four pieces of artillery and another regiment of infantry to make this place up to the Hanover Ferry secure."[41]

Based on such solid intelligence, this suggestion was followed, and the Federal force was augmented enough to make it formidable. On May 27, the Lancers played a major role in the Union victory at the Battle of Hanover Court House. Tom Smith saw his first combat that day, as he relates in the following letter:

Hanover Court House, Virginia
May 28th 1862

Dear Brother

We came in from Picket on Monday [May 26] Afternoon at 6 o'clock. It was Raining verry hard, and continued so until 10 o'clock on Tuesday morning. We were wet through when we came in, so we built fires and set at them all night. We had to keep turning continually, first our Back, and then our Face, to the fire, to keep the shakes off of us. But it was impossible to keep Dry, it Rained so hard.

The ballance of our Regiment, consisting of 7 Companies who were not on Picket went out scouting and Reconoitering on Monday. They drove in the Rebel Pickets taking one prissoner and shooting one. Our Colonel made a narrow escape of being shot as a ball Grazed his Cheek. The shot came from the woods, as they galloping along the road in chase of the Pickets.

On Tuesday morning [May 27] at day Break, we had two days rations served out to us and were ordered to saddle our Horses and take nothing along but our canteens Haversacks and Gum Coats.[42] (By the way I should tell you that we have had to throw away all our Cloathing and Blankets except one change of under shirts one blanket, which we use for a Saddle Blanket. Our Over Coat and Gum Coat. By Order of Col. Rush) We went out by Squaddrons in different directions. Our Squaddron went off first. We went to the Right and Travelled 10 miles, when we came to a Place whare three Roads met. There were two Rebbel cavalry pickets but they Galloped off. We came in right toward them and then our Captain came up to us to go on and Reconoiter the woods ahead. We went up to within 300 Yards of the woods when the First Platon of Company C went through while we halted. They had not been gone ten minutes when we heard Firing ahead and I with 3 men were sent in to see where they were. We went through at a Gallop and when we came out on the other side we met Lieutenant Leves[43] with his Platton comming back. He told us that he came out of the woods there was a party of about 30 Rebbel Cavalry drawn up in front of them across the road. They fired a volley at Leves' party without doing any harm when they skedaddled down the Road with Leves after them. But he was afraid to follow them far for fear of having his Retreat cut off. I went back and Reported, when we all came through the woods. Deployed as skirmishers and sent a messenger back to Col. Rush for further orders. By this time we could hear Firing for miles through the woods to our left and soon heard artillery and vollies of musketry in the Neighborhood of Hanover Court House and knew that a general engagement was going on. Col. Rush sent word back to us, to make for Hanover, with all Haste. Which we did by taking a Bye Road, over the Fields, and through the Woods. We had 5 miles to travel, and when we reached there, the Enemy had retreated and our Regiment was about starting in pursuit of them. We joined in. The 5th Regulars took one Road and we took another, we chased them across the Pamunkey River taking about 60 Prisoners, and then cut down the Bridge and returned to Hanover which we reached at 9 o'clock p.m.[44]

This morning our Company was sent out on a Road (That had not yet been Scouted) to scout the woods, and cut down a Bridge on the Pamunkey. We reached the Bridge, and learnt from some Niggers that a party of Rebbles had crossed about a half hour before we got thare. Our Company drew up on this side of the Bridge and I was sent with three men to Reconoiter on the other side. I stationed one man about 100 yards from the Bridge where the Road took a sharp turn to the left and another man 100 yards further on where it took a turn to the Right. On both sides of the Road thare was a deep Ravine with thick woods, and a heavy groath of under brush. Sam Boyer[45] and I, went on up the Road, which ran straight for a good distanse. And after going about 500 yards we came to a Farm on the Right (There was a heavy Thunder Shower at this time and the rain was almost Blinding)—was a large wheat field and on looking across it I seen a Head making for the Barn, which was on the Road about 200 yards ahead. We kept on up the Road behind the Hedge Fense and when within 20 yards of the barn another Rebble came in sight, close on us, makeing for the Barn. I aimed my Pistole, spirred my Gallant Nag forward and cried out drop that Gun or die. He Dropped his Gun through up his hands and cried I surrender. The other one on seeing us disappeered after into the Barn. We were going after him, when Furnace[46] came up and would not let me go as the man I caught told us that the Woods were full of them, on the other side of the Field. We went back to the Bridge, cut it down, and then Returned to Camp.[47]

Our Infantry, Cavelry, Scouts and Pickets, have been fetching in Prisoners all last night, and today. We Poor Devils in the ranks have no means of knowing how many were killed wounded or taken Prisoner. But I should judge from what I have seen and heard that we have about

1500 to 2000 prisoners of the killed and wounded I cant say anything about them.[48] If there is any thing in the Papers about it, I wish you would let me know the Particulars. By the way do you send me any Papers lately. If so you had better not send any more as I have only Received two Papers in the last Five Weeks. I must now close as it is getting dark. This sheet of Paper I tore out of a Ledger that I found on the Battlefield. It would have done your eyes good to have seen the various Articles that were left laying topsy turvey through their camps and over the Battle Field. But the infantry get all the Plunder as we are not allowed to dismount to pick up anything and the way I got this I stuck my lance in it tore out a couple of sheets and throwed it away againn. Give my love to all the Family or any other friends.

Your affectionate brother

Tom

The Lancers did well at Hanover Court House. The Federal force accomplished its objective of locating the Rebel flank and destroying the bridges over the Pamunkey. Porter commended the role of Rush's men in rounding up Confederate prisoners. One Regular recorded, "On the left stood, formed in a long line across the field, the 6th Pennsylvania Cavalry, then armed with lances . . . and making a fine display, reminding me of the engravings I had seen once of the Mexican cavalry at the war of 1848."[49]

Col. Gouverneur K. Warren of the 5th New York Infantry, who commanded the expedition to the bridge over the Pamunkey River, also praised the performance of the troops under him, stating, "Thrown together as my command was for the first time I have special reason to speak of the promptness and energy with which the different commanders obeyed my orders and seconded me in all my endeavors to carry out [my] instructions." Warren also pointed out the toll that this campaigning took on the regiment's horses: "Two of Colonel Rush's horses gave out and died from exhaustion on the pursuit toward the Pamunkey. . . ." Chaplain Gracey pointed out: "This was the first engagement in which any part of our regiment was recognized as being a participant, and is so mentioned in the report of Colonel Rush to Governor Curtin. The 6th regiment was sent on the extreme right of the advance, and by its active demonstrations in that quarter, served to distract the attention of the enemy from our main infantry column. We were under fire most of the day, but no opportunity offered for the regiment to be used in the charge."[50]

Rush noted, "The regiment was under fire for the first time, and all the officers and men behaved most gallantly."[51] Tom Smith commented, as well, to his brother Joe:

Wednesday May 28th 1862

We were in the saddle at 5 o'clock this morning, and started out to Reconiter the Enemies Position who are said to be in strong force about here. We have one Battery of Artillery, and 2 Regiments of Infantry, with us[52] and the rest of our forces, are drawn up in line of battle, about three miles to our Rear. I think that we must have a force of about Ten Thousand men here at Pressent, as we Received Reenforsements Yesterday. We have drove in the Enemies outer Pickets, and are now laying along the Road, while our Scouts are out Reconoitering. As I write this I am sitting against a Post at a Junction of two Roads. On the Post are two boards, one points to Richmond 13 miles. The other one points to Ashland 5 miles.

Camp near Old Church Thursday May 29th 1862

We got the Order Forward, March yesterday at 10 o'clock and started off at a gallop as the Rebbles were Retreating. We chased them across a Stream of water about 5 miles, burnt the bridges and a Railroad Bridge and cut the Telegraph wires. We took 32 Prisoners including 7 Cavelrymen.[53] One of the Cavelry fired 3 shotts at Lieutenant Morrow of Company B at a distance of 5 yards, but done no harm. We returned to Hanover at six o'clock p.m. Having travelled about 40 mile, and Being in the saddle 14 hours. We then got Orders to Return to our camp near Old Church. Without Dismounting, which was 16 miles distant we Reached here at 11 o'clock p.m. Both our Horses and ourselves completely worn out with Fatigue. We lost 37 Horses out of the Regiment while gone. They were run to death and even my Gallant Nag showes the Effects of Being over exposed and his Back is all Raw. He will not be able to ride again for a Week at Least. I think that we are agoing out on another Expedition today as they are cooking 3 days' Rations this Morning. They are now picking up our mail, so I must close. Give my love to all the Family and all Inquiring Friends. I have just Received the Press of May 23rd which is a reel treat as I have not seen a Philadelphia Paper for some time. I suppose you sent it.

Tom

The campaigning Smith so longed for took its toll on the 6th Pennsylvania. In his report to Governor Curtin, Rush stated, "This ten days' scout was a very hard one, though we lost no men. Thirty-four horses were killed or maimed." The Confederates abandoned Ashland on the twenty-ninth and retreated toward Richmond. On the thirtieth, the Lancers made a reconnaissance toward Ashland, where they took a number of prisoners and burned a railroad bridge. During the course of the expedition, the Lancers took eighty prisoners and eighteen horses, good work for a regiment seeing its first action.[54]

In his next letter home, Smith provided his family with tremendous insight into the daily routine of a Civil War cavalryman during the Peninsula campaign. He included part of a diary that he kept.

[undated]

Dear Sister

Having nothing to do, I thought I would try and write you a few lines to you. But now that I have got paper and pencil out, I have got nothing to write about. However I must try and waste a sheet of paper or two, and if it dont interest you, it will give me something to do. So here goes.

Your letter of the 5th Inst, came to hand in due time, as also did Joes two letters of the 4th and 5th Inst, and two Papers which Joe sent me. The Letters I have Read over untill I know them by Hart, and the Papers I have Read through, news, Editorials, advertisements, and all. You want to know if I have any ideas down this way. Well I have a few which I will proceed to give to you forthwith.

Idea 1st. That Richmond is going to be taken.

Idea 2nd. That it will not be taken so soon, nor so easy, as some People think it will.

Idea 3rd. That it will be taken by Siege, and not by storme, as some People think. (Little Mac is now throwing up Entrenchments, and Planting Siege Guns along our lines).

Idea 4th. That it will be a longer Siege, than the Siege of Yorktown was. So much for Richmond.

Idea 5th. That this laying around Camp with nothing to do but take care of one Horse is a verry Lazy Life.

Idea 6th. That if they dont soon give us something to do, I will do something desperate. For instance Saddle up my Horse some dark night stele out from Camp, and go Scoutting on my own Hook, Get caught, brought back, and court martialled. Wouldnt that be Exciting. I think that is about the last idea I have got.

You want to know about my helth. Well I am as harty as a Buck, the only thing that troubles me, is a better appetite that our Rations allow.

Joe wants to know how I get on so many Scouting parties. The Sorrels are the most wiry set of Horses in the Regiment,[55] and I suppose for that reason we are chosen for scoutting, as it is verry hard on the Horses. I always get on the advance guard, because I have one of the best and most Sagacious Horses in the Company and our Officers know that I like it.

I dont think that our Lances will ever be of any use in this war unless we should get a chance to charge in an open Field. In that case, they would be a most Powerful weapon. The Day after the Battle at Hanover Court House, a company of the 5th Regulars took some prisoners in through our Camp. The 5th Boys were pushing the Rebs about Running away so hard, when one of the Rebs remarked, it wasnt you we run from, it was them fellows with them long Poles. So far the Speer has proved to be the best weapon we have got.

I have just received the Philadelphia Inquirer of June 9th from Joe.

Diary of Camp Life
Friday June 6th 1862

Raining untill 4 o'clock p.m. when the Sun made its apperance onse more. Had several light showers through the night. I was on Stable Guard at night. Received a letter from Joe today Dated June 4th with several scraps of news in it.

Saturday June 7th

The Sun came out Bright and Early in the morning. Had a heavy Thundershower at 2 p.m. which lasted 2 hours. Nothing to do but take care of our selves and our Horses. Mailed a letter to Joe.

Sunday June 8th

Cloudy in the morning but cleared up soon. Had a dismounted Regimental inspection of arms, amunition &c. at 11 a.m. Received a Letter from Joe, dated June 5th, with a map of Virginia, and scraps of news enclosed. Short of rations, 5 crackers 1 cup of Rice soup and 2 cups of coffee without sugar.

Monday June 9th

Clear and verry warm. Had one cracker and a cup of coffee for Breakfast. At 10 a.m. had a cup of Boiled Rice Salt and water. At 10$^{1}/2$ a.m. the Regiment Saddled up and went out Foraging for Horse Feed. We scoured the country for six miles around, but could not find a grain of corn or a Blade of Fodder. We returned to Camp, at 4 p.m. having rode about 25 mile. Our waggons came in at 5 p.m. with a small lot of corn and provisions. We had 18 crackers a piece served out to us for 2 Days Rations. Our Horses got 2 quarts of corn apiece. At 8 p.m. we got a cup of bean soup and a half pound of fresh Beef. I was on Stable Guard at night. It commensed raining at midnight. I Received a Letter Dated June 5th from Susan today. Also The Philadelphia Inquirer of June 3rd and New York Tribune of June 4th from Joe.

Tuesday June 10th

A verry cold disaggreble and Rainey day. Nothing to do. The Third and Fourth Squadrons went out before Day Light.

Wednesday June 11th

We were called up at 4 o'clock a.m. and ordered to Saddle up light, to go for forrage. In 15 minutes we were in the saddle, and on the way we struck into the woods north of our camp, and travelled about 4 mile through woods, swamps, and fields when we came upon barns with some corn fodder in it. We bundled it onto our Horses and returned to Camp at 8 a.m. Rations due and none in camp. We got a cup of coffee and 2 crackers for Breakfast. No Dinner. At 6 p.m. got a cup of coffee at 7 p.m. 4 Waggon loads of corn arrived, and we were told that the Provision train would not arrive until the next morning. I got some corn Parched it in a mess pan, and had a first rate supper. It was clear and verry warm today. Heared cannonading on the left, late in the afternoon. The third and fourth squadrons returned to camp at 6 p.m. They had been scouting and Reconoitering, five mile beyond Hanover Court House.

Thursday June 12th

We got two days Rations of crackers this morning. Had bean soup and Pork for dinner.

Susan you must not think that in writing this Diary I do it to complain for it is not so. I do it as a mere pass time and I know that our short Rations can not be helped. The Roads are so bad and there are so many to supply.

Give my love to all the Family.
Yours affectionately Tom

P.S. I am begging again. Ask Mother if she can spare me another Dollar. I hope by the time that is gone we will get paid.

P.S. Enclosed I send you a couple of Genuine Sesesh shin plasters.[56]

Tom's predictions about the success of the Peninsula campaign were remarkably accurate. He correctly assessed McClellan's failure and also correctly predicted that Richmond would only be taken by siege, proven by Ulysses S. Grant's strategy for winning the war, which involved a protracted siege of Petersburg leading to the cutting of supplies to Richmond.

Also, Smith's affinity for the lance is interesting. While he was obviously enamored of the weapon, the lance was not terribly popular with the men of the regiment, and it was the subject of much jest in the ranks of the Army of the Potomac.[57]

McClellan's grand infantry assault on Richmond began after the Battle of Hanover Court House. A series of battles for Richmond commenced on May 31, 1862, when Confederate general Joseph E. Johnston attacked McClellan at Seven Pines, a few miles east of Richmond. Johnston was badly wounded in this battle, and his place was taken by Gen. Robert E. Lee.

As these battles raged, the Lancers were sent on a series of scouting missions, gaining more experience in the field. On June 12, the Confederate cavalry chieftain, Brig. Gen. J. E. B. Stuart, set off on a raid to reconnoiter the Federal army's position. Swinging out in a large looping arc, Stuart rode around the entire Federal army. Most of the 6th Pennsylvania was sent to pursue Stuart's troopers. Cooke failed, much to the frustration of his men. Capt. Emlen Carpenter of Company E bitterly noted, "Gen. [Cooke] did not attach much importance to the [first reports of the raid] thinking it was only a foraging party, never dreaming in his listlessness that [Stuart] would have the audacity to attack him. . . . The whole affair was a . . . disgraceful failure on the part of Cooke to prevent it. . . . I hope he will do better next time."[58]

McClellan continued his slow advance until his army was within sight of the church steeples of Richmond. The stage was now set for the series of battles that have become known as the Seven Days.

Camp Near Richmond
June 17th 1862

Dear Jenny

We have had quite stirring times about here for the last three or Four days. Last Thursday at 5 p.m. I went on Regimental Guard. On Friday at 2 p.m. some of our waggons, which had been to the White House[59] for provisions, came in and told us that part of the train had been captured by the Rebs, at Old Church and that the Rebels had come in force, from three Different Directions, and surrounded a Squaddron of the 5th Regulars who were on Picket at Old Church and cut them all to pieces. Saddle up was Blown, and our Brigade were drawn up in line of Battle, about a mile from Camp. The Regimental Guards were dismissed to their Companeys and Ordered to Pack the waggons, saddle our Horses, and be Prepaired for a Retreat in case the Rebs advanced our way. At 6 p.m Reenforsements of Infantry and Artillery arrived, and took the Place of our Cavelry, who Returned to Camp Fed their Horses and Packed their Saddles. At 8 p.m. the Cavelry started off again and we Guards had to stay in Camp with the teams. We kept the Horses saddled and the teams Hiched up all night. On Satturday we mooved about one mile and stayed there untill Sunday morning, when we mooved the Camp Equippage and all the waggons and Horsses about 3 miles further. We stayed there untill 12 o'clock and then Returned to our old Camp, as we heard that our Brigade were coming home again. When we got back to Camp we put up the Picket Ropes, and Officers Tents, and they got to work and cooked a Good Dinner for the men of our Company. They got back about 6 o'clock p.m. and I tell you the way they went into the Pork and Bean soup was a caution.[60]

The Rebble Force is variously estimated from 1,000 to 3,000 cavelry and 6 pieces of Light Artillery. They surrounded Captain Royals Squaddron at

Old Church. Captain Royal[61] called his men together formed them in line and made a charge at the Rebs to try and cut his way through. Royal was wounded in 5 places. 3 Saber cuts 1 Pistol Shot and 1 carbine shot which shows how Desperately we fought. Two thirds of his men were either killed or taken Prisoner. The ballance of them made their escape. Royals wounds are not mortal.

Lieutenant Morrow of Company B and Lieutenant Davis[62] acting Quartermaster both of our Regiment were taken Prisoner or killed. They with their two servents were returning from the White House and when near Old Church they met a teamster, who told them that they were fighting ahead. The servents turned and went back to White House and Davis and Morrow went ahead, and that was the last seen or heard of them. The Rebs destroyed a Large quantity of our stores and burnt a Great many of our waggons along the Road. At one time they were within 5 miles of the White House. One of our Ambulances and the Driver, Wm. Calhoun of Company K were captured by the Rebs.

The squaddrons changed so that was the reason of our Return to the Regiment. We are now in Squaddron with Company D. Captain Starr is our Squaddrons officer. We are in the 5th Squaddron.

I received Susan's letter of June 12th yesterday. Also the money Enclosed. I am verry sorry to hear that Susan is sick, and I hope that when this reaches home she will be better. No more at Pressent. Give my best love to all the Family.

Yours affectionately
Tom

P.S. Give my best love to Cousin Louisa. I wish I was there to see her. Tell her to write to me that I would be glad to hear from her.

Tom

TURN OVER

Dear Joe

I wish you would look around Town and see if you can find any Cavelry Sergents Shevrons ready made and let me know how much they are. The sergents of our Company wish to get them all alike. We will want 5 or 6 sets of them.

They are made with 3 pieces of yellow Braid sowed on to a piece of Dark Blue Cloth in this shape >>>. You will be likely to see them at Horstmens Milatary Store.[63] Write soon and give me a description of your trip to the White House.

Yours & c.

Tom

Smith and his comrades no longer lacked for action. In fact, the Lancers received credit for locating the retreating Southern column and for giving the Federals the chance to bring it to bay.[64] They would remain integrally involved in the balance of McClellan's Peninsula campaign. Smith was also promoted to sergeant on June 1, as he had predicted to his brother Joe.[65] It meant new duties: Sergeants were in charge of squads of men, typically in groups of about twenty. They were responsible for maintaining order and discipline, cleanliness, and teaching tactics to the enlisted men. While on the march, they were to see that the men did not straggle or fall out, and they were to inspect the horses and equipment of the men.[66] These were even more important duties than he had as a corporal, and he was up to the task.

Camp Near Mechanicsville Virginia

Friday, June 20th 1862

Dear Father

We left our old Camp on Wednsday morning 18th inst, in Company with the 1st, 5th and 6th Regulars, the 8th Penna, and the 1st New York, (all cavalry) and marched about 5 miles and encamped near Gaines Mills.

On Thursday morning 19th Inst, the 1st Squaddron, Companys B and G and the 2nd Sqaddron, Companys C and I were detached from the Brigade and ordered to report to Gen. McCall's Division at Mechanicsville.[67] We reached here about noon, and the 1st Squaddron were sent out on picket, and we encamped in the woods about one mile from Mechanicsville. By climbing a tree, we can see the Smoke of the enemies camp coming out of the woods on the other side of the Chickahominy. We can see their Baterys, and with a Glass we can see them digging their last Ditch. Their pickets are within three quarters of a mile of our Camp. This morning one of Company B's Pickets traded his canteen of coffee, for a canteen of whiskey, with one of the Rebel Pickets.

Professor Lowes Balloon and Gas apperatis is rite by our Camp.[68] They were working at it all night, and got it filled this morning. About 11 o'clock am the Balloon went up, when the Rebs Fired a Shell at it, which passed over it and fell back of the Woods in the Rear of our Camp. We hauled the Balloon in and carried it further back out of range, when it went up again. The Rebs Fired a Few more shell at it, but finding it was out of range they ceased Fireing.

In Camp Near Gaines Mills
Sunday June 22nd 1862

While writing the foregoing lines the day before Yesterday, we were ordered to saddle up and go on Picket. We went through Mechanicsvill, and down to the Chickahominy River whare the Virginia Central Rail Road Crosses that stream. The 1st Penna Rifles[69] were with us. They were posted along the Roads. Our pickets and the Rebel Pickets could talk together, and on the Bridge they would come over and trade caps and other small things with our men. A few miles further to our left, a party of our Men were building a Bridge and in the morning the Rebbels opened two Batterys on them. Our Batterys returned their Fire, and then the Rebbels directed their Fire at our Batterys, so they kept up a Regular Artillery Duel all Day. One of our men who was working on the Bridge told me that out of 27 shells that the Rebbels threw at them only one burst, and that their aim was so bad that they never stopped our men from working.

The Rebbel Pickets at the Rail Road Bridge told us that a shell from one of our Parrot Guns Burst big and killed General Lees Horse under him.

On Saturday at 5 p.m. Company H came out and relieved us, and brought orders for us to Return to Camp. The vacencies of commissioned Officers in the Regiment were Filled up.

When Joe gets home again tell him to write and tell me all about his trip to the White House. I should like verry much to get over there and see him, but I dont know when he will be there or how long he will stay. Our Camp is about 25 miles from the White House, by the Road our Teams travel.

I was appointed sergent yesterday in place of McGratton. He was reduced for giving the wrong countersign, the countersign was New

Orleans and he gave to some of the sentries California some New York and some New Orleans.

I received your letter of the 12th on Sunday also *Forneys War Press*. Write soon again. My love to all the family.

Tom

On June 25 the Seven Days Battles commenced, a series of ferocious attacks by Robert E. Lee, intended to drive McClellan's army from the gates of Richmond. Lee won each of the battles except the last one, fought at Malvern Hill near the banks of the James River. During the great fight at Gaines' Mill on June 27, the Federal cavalry made its first mark in the war, making a massed, mounted charge on the victorious Confederate infantry. The Lancers supported that charge, to their fame and glory, protecting a battery of Regular artillery from capture. Some of them caught the fire of the charge and joined it.[70] For some unknown reason, Tom failed to mention this fact in a letter to his brother Joe on July 9, 1862.

Also, on July 6, 1862, the Lancers were assigned a different mission. Special Order No. 195, issued by McClellan, provided in part, "The 6th Pennsylvania Cavalry will be organized as a corps of guides, and will by frequent reconnaissances and scouts, be kept fully instructed as to the roads and character of the county. In case of a movement, [Brig.] General [George] Stoneman will send detachments from this regiment to guide the different divisions."[71] This definite change in the mission of the Lancers was important duty for an inexperienced regiment gaining respect in the eyes of the army's high command. Smith was especially fond of scouting duty and must have enjoyed this particular assignment. In a letter of July 9, he describes his return from such a scouting mission.

Fort Monroe Virginia
July 9th 1862

Dear Joe

On the morning of the 4th we mooved up to fortress Monroe and went into Barracks. On the 7th we got Orders to saddle up and go down to [Harrison's] Landing, to embark on vessels, to go up the James River, to McClellans armey, and join our Regiment. We stayed at the Landing all day, and the Regulars and one of our Companeys got Embarked. At dark the rest of us went back to the Barracks.

Those who were Embarked were anchored out in the River untill this morning, when they came in and now they are unloading again.

General Burnside[72] is here with his forses, and from all apperenses I think that he is going off on some new Expedition. It is verry probably that we will go with him.

I have not heard anything Deffinite about our Regiment yet, but I think that they are safe with McClellans armey.

I have been verry sick since the 4th Inst when I was taken with severe cramps in the stomach which lasted all night. And sinse then I have had a bad Pain in my Kidneys and at times if I moove my Boddy the least bit, I suffer the most Excrutiating pains. I am under the hands of a good Doctor, and if our company stays here a few Days longer, (which I think they will) I will be able to leave with them.[73]

I wish you would write soon, as I have not had a Letter from home sinse I Received Susans Letter of June 12th and if you have wrote any they are with the Regiment.

They are firing a Sallute now at the Fort (5 pm). They say it is in Honor of President Lincoln who is Landing here.

No more at pressent. Give my love to all the Family. Hopeing that this may find you all as well as I expect to be in a few days I Remain

Your Affectionate Brother
Tom

P.S. I wish you would ask Mother if she can spare me another Dollar. My appetite is completely gone. I cant eat Hard crackers any more. And while we stay here, if I had a little money, I think a change of diet would do me good.

Smith still did not mention the exploits of the Lancers, who had received negative reports about their performance at Gaines' Mill. Some accused them of cowardice for breaking and running from the field after the repulse of the Fifth U.S. Cavalry, and these accusations made it into the Philadelphia newspapers, much to the anger and chagrin of the Lancers. One trooper took great pains to quash those rumors in a letter to the editor, writing indignantly, "Any man who was on the field and says that the Lancers ran away, or that they flinched under the heavy fire, or that they did not march off the field in good order, and slowly, and that they were not the last to leave, simply lies."[74]

Harrisons Landing
July 25

Dear Sister

I Received your letter yesterday, and having time on the way, I thought I should answer it. The armey is laying verry quiet at pressent, and there is no excitement of any kind, except a little Cannonading on the River now and then, or an occasional Skirmish between the Cavelry Pickets and Scouting parties.

Last night Lieutenant Abe Price with twenty men was ordered to report to Gen. Heintzelman's Quarters at 8 o'clock pm.[75] Heintzelman ordered us to take the Long Bridge Road and go as far as a Church, (which is situated about six and a half miles from our lines and three miles from our outter Pickets) and see if we could see anything of the Rebbels. We went as far as the Church and Halted, when Lieut. Price and I went about 50 yds further to a turn in the Road. We seen a Rebbel Picket Guard of three men about 20 yds off. One of them immediately wheeled his Horse and Galloped off to Report to their mane guard, and the other two fired their Carbines at us, one ball struck the ground under our Horses, and the other one passed directly under our Horses necks and lodged in the fense on our left. We fired five Pistol Shots after them as they Galloped off, and then as they Galloped off, and then as we were so far from our Pickets with such a small forse, we turned and Galloped off as hard as we could go untill we got inside of our pickets not knowing how near the Enemy might be on our Right and Left. We were afraid of being cut off. We got back to Camp at 2 o'clock p.m. pretty well tired out, having rode about 20 miles through the Hot Sun.

You want to know my opinion of McClellens late movements. Well it is my oppinion and the oppinion of all with whom I have conversed on the subject that McClellen has been Defeated and Gained a victory both at the same time. That is he was Defeated before Richmond before the fighting commensed, and he knew it. He knew several days before the fighting commensed, from the moovements of the Enemey that they intended to attack him with an overwelming forse, and he knew that if he attempted to hold his position that his armey would be overpowered by numbers and annihilated. Therefore he determined to change his position (which he commensed two days before the fighting began by Removing his stores at the White House and also his heavy siege trains) to the James River, and with the assistence of the gun boats hold his position here untill reinforsed, and there is where he gained a great victory by saving his armey from a complete rout. Some vilonous Scoundrel in Banks Armey a reporter of the *Philadelphia Press* Published a letter in that Paper that the men of McClellens armey had lost confidence in him. Why the men fairley idollise him and are more eager to be led into battle by him than ever whenever he makes an appearance among the soldiers he is greated by cheres on every Hand.

Change her is verry scarse, if a man has a dollar note he has to buy the whole of it out, as they will not give specia change for notes. And it is mighty little we can get for a dollar. Bread 20 cts a loaf and it weighs less than a Pound. Cheese 60 cts to 75 cts per lb. Brown sugar 25 cts white sugar 30 to 35 cts per lb.

I received Susans letter a few days sinse, and this letter will have to do for both of you. Write soon and let me know if Mother and Susan are getting better. Give my love to all the Family.

Your brother
Tom

P.S. Tell Joe and Bob not to go a soldiering unless they are drafted, for this Hot Sun down here will Kill off these new Recruits verry fast.

Tom

Smith's perceptions about the Peninsula campaign are deep; McClellan was defeated primarily through his own caution and unwillingness to commit his entire army to a decisive battle. Although McClellan saved his command from the perceived threat and protected his base of operations along the James River, the entire campaign was a strategic defeat since he was driven back from the gates of the Confederate capital by Lee's newly christened Army of Northern Virginia.

The Lancers remained in camp at Harrison's Landing until July 24, doing guide and scout duty on a daily basis. The regimental historian noted that "with this exception, our stay here was devoid of all service, and the monotony of camp life in midsummer uninterrupted."[76] Finally, on August 5, the regiment marched to Harrison's Landing to cover the withdrawal of the Army of the Potomac from the Peninsula, presumably for other fields. On August 7, Smith took time to write to his brother Joe during a rest stop at Westover. Tom offers an interesting insight into the callous attitudes of the regiment's officers toward the enlisted men.

Westover

August 7th 62

Dear Joe

I Received your letter some time ago and was verry glad to hear from Home. The weather is so verry hot and the flies so bad down here that I dont feel much like writing, and that is the reason I have neglected to answer your Letter sooner.

On the night of the 31st July I was on guard, and abought midnight the Rebbels on the other side of the River commensed throwing shell over at us verry Rappidly. At first they all passed over our camp, but toward the last there was a great many Lodged in and around our camp. We had one man killed. As soon as there Guns opened on them they left. The next day our Troops made a landing on the other side and made a splened Bonfire of a Dwelling and out Buildings where the Rebbels had been in the Habit of congregating. They are also clearing the woods away from along the water. We have now a pretty strong forse over there.

The day before yesterday we heard Heavy Fireing in the direction of Malvern Hill. It commensed about Day Break and lasted about 3 hours. Afflerwards learnt that our Gun Boats shelled the Rebbels from Malvern Hill and our men took possession of it capturing one Battery and taking some 200 Prisoners. I see it stated in the Papers that the Soldiers, sinse they have been here get Fresh Beef 4 times per week, that they are served with Cabbage Tomattos Potatoes and other vegatables and that they get Bread instead of crackers. Now sinse we have been here, we have had fresh Beef 4 times and one time it was so stinking when we got it, that we dug a hole and burried it right away.

As for Vegetables, the only thing of the kind we have had sinse we were here is Potatoes and only 5 Rations of them 3 Potatoes to a Ration. Bread we have never received a loaf. Some of the Sutlers have put up ovens, and got to baking bread, they bake it into 7 oz Loves and sell it at 15 cts per Loaf.

Now some of the Regiments do get what the Papers say they do, but not in such large quanties, and there are some Regiments that even get fresh bread all the time. And I know that all the Regiments get a variety of Vegetables in small quantities. Now the only reason why we dont get these things is becaus our Officers are to lazy and careless to go to the trouble to get them.

But there is one thing that they aint too lazy to get, that is wines jelleys Preserves Liquors Orranges Lemmons and other Delicacies which are contributed by the ladies for the Benefit of the Sick. These articles they draw in Large quantities but the sick men never get a taste of them, while the Officers tables are allways loaded with them. This I know to be a fact for the Boxes are Labled Hospital Stores and I have seen them opened. What would those kind Folk think if they knew to what use those articles were put, which they intended for the sick and wounded soldiers. I say shame on such Officers. They ought to be shown up to the world for their meanness. The majority of our Officers are a set of Arristocratic Fops, and care no more or have no more feelling for the men in the Ranks than so many dogs.

There are now over 5 months pay Due us, while all the other Regiments down here have been paid off up to the 1st of July. They get their pay every 2 months. On this late retreat the men lost nearly every thing they had, in other Regiments they Drew new articles Blankets Knap Sacks Haversacks Canteens clothing &c and were not charged one cent for them. While we had to pay full price for every article that we drew and we lost every thing. Now wetherer the Officers can gain any thing by this or not I cant say, but it is either that or else they are two lazy to go to the troble to have it arranged in the Propere manner.

It is a Gross Piece of Imposition on the men many of us whoom have familys and cannot afford to loose so much. If we keep on at this rate it will take $2/3$ of our pay to keep us in cloaths.

I am verry glad to hear that Mother is getting better. I recive your papers verry regularly now. I have Received 4 this week. I think 2 of them were from Fathere. No more at pressent. Write soon.

Yours Affectionately

Tom

The Army of the Potomac began withdrawing from the Peninsula on
August 11. The Fifth Corps went to the aid of Maj. Gen. John Pope's Army
of Virginia, which was then facing Lee's army in Culpeper County.

Hampton
Aug 20th/62

Dear Brother

On last Monday a week ago they commensed to ship Troops from
Harrisons Landing, and they were shipping them night and day untill
Friday night. On Satturday morning when we got up every vessel, Gun
Boats and all had disappeared from the River. On Thursday morning the
Ballance of the Forses with the waggons, commensed to moover. They took
the Charles City Road, which keeps pretty close to the James River all the
way to Williams Burgh. There were 2 squaddrons of our Regiment
Detached 1 Squaddron to Gen Porter and 1 squaddron to Gen Franklin.[77]
The other 3 squaddrons were Detailed to the Guard the waggons and help,
and hurry them through. Our squaddron was the Rear Guard of the
waggon train. We left camp on Satturday at 8 am and marched 12 miles.
We then encamped untill Sunday morning to Leave the waggons pass
us. On Sunday morning at 8 am we started again and marched to the
Chickahominy a distance of 15 miles which we reached at 12 o'clock. We
halted here for 2 hours and then started again and marched to Williams
Burgh a distance of 14 mile which we reached at dark. We layed at
Williams Burgh untill 1 o'clock on Monday when we started again and
marched to Yorktown, which we reached at dark. We stayed at York Town
untill 1 o'clock on Tuesday when we started and marched to this Place a
distance of 20 miles which we reached at 7 o'clock pm.

I think as soon as they can furnish transportation we will be shipped and
go up the Rapahonock and join Popes Armey.[78]

I received your letter of the 16th this morning. I am verry sorry to hear of
Mothers continued bad Health. I hope that when this Reaches home that
Mother and Jane will both be better.

When you write again give me the Particulars of the cause of Susan
leaving Carlisle so soon. I am sorry to hear that Robert[79] has enlisted,
Especially so in Infantry, as I am afraid that he will never be able to
stand marching, and carry a musket and knap sack. It would have been

much better for him if he had enlisted in Cavelry. No more at pressent. Write soon.

Your Affectionate Brother

Tom

P.S. Give my best love to Mother and tell her that I Received those 2 Dollars. Give my love to all the Family.

Tom

Around August 15, the balance of the 6th Pennsylvania pulled out of the area around Hampton and sailed to Washington. Lee's army was operating in the central part of the state, looking for an opportunity to destroy Pope's army, an opportunity that finally presented itself at the Battle of Second Bull Run on August 30 and 31. In the interim, the Lancers ended their role in the Peninsula campaign quietly, serving as part of the garrison defending Washington, D.C. Their days were spent scouting and picketing, waiting for more interesting duty to come along. On August 23, while the regiment was en route to Washington, Smith found time to pen his last letter home during the Peninsula campaign.

New Market Bridge
Aug 23/62

Dear Sister

We mooved our Camp the day before yesterday from Hampton back to New Market Bridge. The same place that we were Encamped last spring. How long we will stay here I cannot tell, but it is verry Likely that we will be Shipped off some place verry soon. It is rumored that we are going to Washington, but I guess there is no trooth in it.

I did not receive Susans letter untill yesterday. I also received 4 Newspapers with it. Susan tells me that Mother had a strike of the Palsy while walking in Market St one evening. I hope that it will leave no bad effects.

You must write soon and let me know how Mother is getting, also let me know about your own Health which Susan tells me is verry Bad. I have no more to say at Pressent, give my Love to all the Family. Write soon.

Your Affectionate Brother

Tom

P.S. Tell Joe that we Received 26 New Recruits the Day before yesterday and that among the number was Wilson Smith of the Union Artillery Guards. He went into Company F.

The Lancers saw action for the first time during the Peninsula campaign, performing well in the missions assigned them. They participated in the combined arms expedition to Hanover Court House and the great mounted charge at Gaines' Mill. Brig. Gen. Philip St. George Cooke wrote of their role at Gaines' Mill: "from the first opening of the fight until its close, after 8 o'clock, the 6th Pennsylvania Cavalry behaved like veterans."[80] In the process, Smith saw his first combat and was promoted to sergeant. His first campaign in the field was a good one, although it is clear from his letters home that he found much of his daily routine boring. Such is the life of a soldier in the field.

No longer green, Smith and the Lancers stood poised to play a significant role in the developing mounted arm of the Army of the Potomac, and they would not have long to wait. In the wake of Pope's defeat at Second Manassas, Lee decided to take the war to the North, and his first great invasion of the North was underway. The remnants of Pope's shattered army and McClellan's Army of the Potomac streamed into the defenses of Washington. As Lee's army moved off into central Maryland, McClellan, again commanding all of the Federal forces, cautiously followed.

CHAPTER THREE

"I Have Been Very Low with the Fever and Ague"

The Maryland Campaign and Severe Malaria

T HE LANCERS CAME NORTH from Hampton and rejoined the Army of the Potomac in the outskirts of Washington, D.C., where they awaited the chance to see action once again. Two companies of the 6th Pennsylvania Cavalry, B and G, were detached from the regiment and sent to serve as headquarters guard for Maj. Gen. William B. Franklin's infantry corps. The balance of the regiment was assigned to the defenses of the capital and brigaded with the 4th Pennsylvania Cavalry. Commanded by Colonel Rush, the small Third Brigade was assigned to the Army of the Potomac's newly formed cavalry division, commanded by Brig. Gen. Alfred Pleasonton. The regimental historian later observed that during this period, "Washington City was never in such a whirl of excitement."[1] By September 5, the "Young Napoleon" knew that the Confederates were advancing into Maryland and took steps to pursue them. On the sixth, McClellan's pursuit began.

Camp Near Washington
Sept 6th/62

Dear Brother

We shipped at Hampton on the First inst, and arrived at Alexandria
at Five O'clock p.m. on the Fourth inst. We got unloaded about
11 O'clock p.m. and mooved out side the town and Encamped there untill
Morning, when we saddled up and marched to Washington crossing the
Long Bridge.[2] We are now Encamped on 7th St. about two miles from
Washington City and opposite to our old camp ground on 14th St. Meredian
Hill. We expect to go into Barracks in a few Days, and Remain here untill

we Recruit up a little, as both the men and Horses are sadly in need of rest. Yesterday afternoon I heared that Col. Collis Zouaves³ were Encamped about 3 miles from here, so I got a pass and went out there to see Bob. I inquired all through the Regiment and found 17 Smiths in it, and among them 5 Bob Smiths but our Bob was not there. I returned to camp somewhat Disappointed at my non success.

When I got back to Camp I found that our mail had arrived, I received Susans letter of Aug 18th, Jennys letter of Aug 25th, Five News Papers, and also that striping with your letter of Aug 30th. The striping is verry fine and of the right stripe.

I heard today that the Corn Exchange Regiment⁴ are Laying at Alexandria, as soon as I can do so, I shall try and get a pass to go there and see Bob. I wish you would write and let me know what company Bob is in.

I am glad to hear that you and Sue were well pleased with your visit to Allentown. No more at pressent. Give my Love to all the Family. Write soon.

Your affectionate brother

Tom

For Joe

If you remember rightly I took sick when I was down at Fort Monroe on the Fourth of July, well after we went up to Harrison's Landing, I wrote that I had regained my health which was not so, the reason of my doing so was because I wanted to ease the mind of Mother and the Rest of the Family in Regaard to me. A few days after we went up there I got the Typhoyed Fever and was in the Hospital for 21 dayes. For 7 days I was Delerious and out my mind. When we left Harrison's Landing I was verry weak but I had to stand the march. The 2nd day of our march I was verry weak and sick about 10 o'clock in the morning I fainted and fell off my Horse for the want of Ambulances which were all full. I was put in a Government waggon and thus I traveled to Fort Monroe. Yesterday was the first Day that I was on duty sinse the 4th Day of July. I feel verry well now, but I am a little week yet. I owe my Recovery entirely to a change of dyet which I have had a chance to Procure sinse I have been Paid off and I intend to spend my money for good and substantial food untill I Regain my Strength, that is if we remain here and I have a chance to do so.

Troops are arriving here all day yesterday and today. Burnsides troops[5] are all here and Popes have been coming all day, and still they come. I dont know what it means, but I do wish that Little Mac was commander in chief. I believe that Popes armey are completely Demoralised, that Break and Run in every Battle they get into.

I have just Received Susans letter of 4th Inst. Tell her to give my Love to all the Folks at Allentown and tell them that I am well.

Smith was very fortunate indeed to have survived typhoid fever. It was "a continual fever of long duration, usually attended with diarrhoea, and characterized by peculiar intestinal lesions, an eruption of small rose spots, and enlargement of the spleen." Because doctors did not know how to cure typhoid fever, it usually was fatal within two weeks of the time that symptoms first appeared.[6]

In the interim, the Army of the Potomac moved out from the ring of forts surrounding Washington and marched into Maryland, searching for Lee's Army of Northern Virginia. Pleasonton's cavalry experienced minor skirmishes on September 9 and 10 as the opposing horsemen jousted for position. While the Lancers were not involved in those skirmishes, they nevertheless accompanied the army's advance into Maryland. A detachment of the regiment, commanded by Maj. George E. Clymer[7] and consisting of Companies B, G, and Smith's I, was assigned as the headquarters detachment of Maj. Gen. William B. Franklin's Sixth Corps.

Thursday
Poolsville, Md
Sept 11th/62

Dear Brother

Last Sunday Evening at 6 o'clock, while in Camp on 7th St near Washington, we got orders to march with 4 days Rationes in our Haversacks and to leave all Sick and Sickly men behind, who were not able to stand an active and hard Campaign. Well we were soon on the Road, and by 11 o'clock we encamped haveing made 12 miles. On Monday morning we started again at Daylight and marched to Rockvill[8] and there encamped. On Monday Evening at 8 o'clock our Company was detached from the Regiment and ordered to report to Gen. Couch[9] at Columbia Cross Road 6 miles distant.

We lost our road and did not reach Gen Couch's Head Quarters untill 4 o'clock on Tuesday morning.

At 7 o'clock a.m. Our Division marched to Tinicum Mills and there we encamped and layed there untill Wednesday morning, when we marched to Poolsville where we are laying right now. 7 o'clock a.m. we expect to leave here Every moment.

And now I am agoing to tell you of a piece of Bad Luck that I had. The Night before last when we got to Tinicum Mills, I went down to the crick to wash. After washing I threw away my old pants and put on a new Pair, and in the watch fob of my Old Pants I left my money Purse with all my money in it, between 14 and 15 Dollars. I had no occasion to use my money untill last evening, when I wanted to buy some bread and felt for my money to pay for it, and found it was gone. I tryed to get leave to go back for it, but they would not give it to me. I guess I would not have found it any way, as when evere we Leave a Camp the Niggers pick up all the old cloathing and Every thing that is left behind. I wish Mother would try and send me a little money, if she it to spare, as I borrowed 2 Dollars from Lieutenant Price[10] last Evening and I wish to return it as soon as possible. No more at pressent. Give my love to all the Family, hoping that you are all as well as I am. I remain

Your affectionate brother

Tom

We are Gen Couches Boddy Guard and we also act as Scouts, Guides, Orderlies and Dispatches for the Division.

On September 13, a detachment of the Lancers, commanded by Lt. Charles L. Leiper, drove off a large force of dismounted Confederate cavalry near Frederick, Maryland. Chaplain Samuel Gracey noted, "Although largely outnumbering his small force, he drove them in confusion, and made some prisoners. The enemy were armed with carbines, and though our men had only the lance and their pistols, by one determined charge, they succeeded in dislodging the enemy, who fled in dismay."[11] The next day, the Lancers watched the Battle of South Mountain rage but took no part in that fight.[12] The Army of the Potomac surged through the South Mountain gaps toward a meeting with Lee's army along the banks of the Antietam Creek.

In the meantime, the Lancers got a taste of the cost of war when they marched through the South Mountain battlefield the day after the struggle. Capt. Robert Milligan noted, "This was the first time I had ever seen a battlefield the day after the fight: it was a horrible, disgusting sight to look upon."[13] The great battle of Antietam came on September 17, the bloodiest day of the American Civil War. McClellan launched a series of disjointed and largely unsuccessful attacks against Lee's vastly outnumbered army, pinned between the Antietam Creek and the Potomac River.

Three stone bridges over Antietam Creek played prominent roles in the battle. Franklin's corps supported Burnside's attacks on the Rohrbach Bridge over the Antietam Creek on the southern end of the battlefield. The corps was not heavily engaged in the fighting, but Gracey noted that "Companies 'B,' 'G,' and 'I' of our regiment, were with General Franklin on this part of the field, and were greatly exposed during all the afternoon."[14] The balance of the regiment participated in a brigade-sized charge intended to take the middle bridge over the Antietam. This charge was successful, but the acting brigade commander, Col. James H. Childs of the 4th Pennsylvania Cavalry, was killed by a solid artillery shot. Captain Milligan observed that the Lancers "made a handsome charge with three other Cavalry Regiments across the stone bridge on the left centre of our position, to support our advanced batteries, and were under a heavy artillery fire for 7 hours."[15] Smith made a passing mention of this fact in a letter to his sister Susan written two weeks later.

On September 19, two days after the battle, Lee pulled his battered army back into Virginia. On the twenty-first, the Sixth Corps marched to the important river-crossing town of Williamsport, Maryland, where it joined Couch's division. Company I of the Lancers stayed with Couch's command. However, Tom Smith had to leave the army with a severe illness, evidently contracted on the Peninsula. He was hospitalized in Chambersburg, Pennsylvania, beginning the worst period of his military service.

Chambersburgh
Oct 4th/62

Dear Sister

I am now in the Franklin Hall Hospital at Chambersburgh. I have been verry low with the Fever and Ague, and also the Rheumatism. But I have got pretty well over the Ague, and am troubled with nothing now, but the

Rheumatism, and a pain at my Heart. I was first sent to the Hospital at Hagerstown, Md, on last Tuesday a week. And on the following Friday I was sent on here, we will be sent on to Harrisburgh, as soon as transportation can be furnished.

I have sent a letter to the orderly sergent of our Company Directing him to send, all letters that come for me, to Joe. I have also directed him to have my descriptive list made out, and sent on. And I wish as soon as Joe receives it he will send it on to me.

I have not received a letter from Home sinse I Received Joe's letter of the 10th of Sept. Did Joe receive my Letter of Sept 11th in it I told him about me loosing my money.

I am treated verry well here, and have almost every Thing that I could wish for. I was on the Battle Field of Antietam and Sharpsburgh as a messenger, and was under fire several times but escaped unhurt. Answere this as soon as you get it, as I am anxious to hear from home. Let me know how Father is getting. I hope that he is well by this time. Give my Love to all the Family.

Your affectionate brother
Tom

Direct your letter to
   Thomas W. Smith, Sergent, Comp. I, 6th Regt. of Penna. V. Cavelry at Franklin Hall Hospital, Chambersburgh, Penna.

While Smith never specifically names his malady, his symptoms point to malaria, presumably contracted in the swamps of the Virginia Peninsula. Unfortunately, many of the Union soldiers were afflicted by the fevers Smith described. For instance, Sgt. Oliver Willets of the 10th New York Infantry of the Fifth Corps also contracted malaria from his proximity to "that fever and ague stream the Chickahominy river."[16] Smith regularly refers to suffering from "ague shakes." Ague was another name for influenza, but no strains of influenza were known to last for the nearly five months Smith spent in various hospitals. Rather, symptoms of malaria commonly included trembling and shivers. Some doctors called it pernicious intermittent fever due to its tendency to recur.

The tone of Smith's letters becomes increasingly desperate and lonely. While not echoing the calls of bugles and cavalry charges, they provide great insight into Smith's thought processes, as he grew increasingly despondent about his inability to shake the lingering effects of the malaria.

Harrisburg

Oct 8th/62

Dear Brother

I left Chambersburg yesterday morning at 8 o'clock, and arrived at the Hospital at Camp Curtin about noon.

This morning I got a pass to come into Town to visit Cousin Louisa. I am now at her House, I got here at 11 o'clock and they had me to stay to Dinner. I like Cousin's Husband verry well, he made me feel at home before I was with him Five Minutes.

Last Sunday while at Chambersburg, Uncle George came over from Strawsburg[17] to see me and on Monday Uncle Neill, and his wife, came over. On Monday I also saw Mr. McClellan, and Fred Sullinger, and George Yow, all from Strawsburg. The Folks at Strawsburg are all well, and send their Love to the Family. Uncle Neill and Uncle George particularly send their Love to Mother. Tell Mother she must write up to Strawsburg.

Joe, have you heard from my company yet, if so write and let me know as soon as Possible. And if you have Received my descriptive list send it to me.

I am at Camp Curtin Hospital Ward 3rd Harrisburg, Penna. Cousins Louisa and Family are all well, and send their Love to you. Tell Susan that she must write to Louisa, or if she dont I will pull her Hair for her, when I come home. And Joe I wish you too would write to Louisa. No more at Pressent. Write soon. Give my Love to all the Family.

Your affectionate brother

Tom

P.S. I have heard that Bobs Regiment was in the Battle of Antietam, let me know if you have heard anything from him.[18]

I have got pretty well over my sickness and begin to feel strong again. But I am still troubled with Rheumatism.

Tom

———

Harrisburg
Oct 15th/62

Dear Father

I Received your letter of the 11th Inst, and am verry glad to hear that you are
getting better. Your letter was the First that I have received from Home
sinse I left Washington. I have not received either Susans, or James letters
from Chambersburg. I suppose that they were sent from there to the
Regiment, and they will come home again.

I am now verry well again except the Rheumatism which sticks to me.

There is nothing of interest going on here so that I have nothing to write
about and you must Excuse this short note. Give my Love to all the Family,
Hoping that this may find you all well I remain

Your affectionate son
Thomas W. Smith

P.S. I have not had one cent of money sinse I left my Company, and I have
had to beg, paper, envelops, postage stamps for every letter that I have
wrote. If it be convenient, I wish you would send me Fifty Cents by Return
of mail, to defray these small expenses.

Tom

———

Harrisburg
Oct 18th/62

Dear Sister

I received your letter of the 10th Inst with Two Dollars enclosed last
evening. Also your letter of the 16th Inst with Two Dollars, an Father letter
of the 16th Inst with Fifty Cents. The Letters that were sent to the Regiment
I think will be safe. But those that were sent to Chambersburg, I dont think
I will ever get, as I sent a letter to Doctor Woolf about them, and he sent
word back that he inquired for them but could learn nothing about them.
However, they may possibly turn up some place yet.

The reason I want my descriptive list is because I cannot get sent away
from here unless I have it. I cannot draw any cloathing without it, or get a
Discharge, or Furlough, or get Paid off, in case the Pay Master should come

around here. So you see, the Descriptive List, is a verry nessessary article to a soldier who is absent from his Regiment.

Dr. Hays the commanding surgeon of the Hospital here, has sent word to the Colonels of all the Regiments of all the men here for their Descriptive Lists. I will write to my Company again for those letters.

I have not much to say, unless that this is the meanest place that I was ever in. The Sick men and Cripples are kept under guard and dare not leave the Hospital without a Pass, while there are a lot of Rebbel Prisoners here, who are allowed the Free Run of the whole Camp (Hard isent it)

Our Fare is Dry Bread and Coffee for Breakfast Boiled Beef Dry Bread and water for Dinner Coffee and Dry Bread for Supper. Louisa and Family are well. I get a Pass and go in there Every Three or Four Days. No more at Pressent. Write soon.

My Love to you and all the Family.
Your affectionate brother
Tom

P.S. I have had an Ague Shake and Fever for the last three days from 12 to 3 o'clock. I had a verry bad one today.

I sent home from Washington if so let me know. My Love to all the Family. Write soon, no more at pressent from your

Brother Tom

As with typhoid fever, the treatment for malaria was often nearly as unpleasant as the illness itself. For severe cases such as Smith's, it generally consisted of the administration of bottles of hot water or heated bricks to the lower extremities, and the administration of opium and quinine in pill form when the patient was well enough to swallow. The patient's diet was closely monitored. Thin soups and tea were dietary staples, as was medicinal brandy. However, if the patient could not keep down food, he would be fed morphine-laced coffee, which was supposed to calm his stomach. Often this would lead to the opposite result. Finally, the treatment protocol required continued administration of quinine, even after the patient's discharge from the hospital.[19] Given the treatment regimen, it is no wonder that Smith often sneaked out of the hospital to find a decent meal at his cousin Louisa's house.

Harrisburg Pa
Oct 23rd/62

Dear Sister

I received your Letter of the 16th Inst on Saturday last and on the Day
before I Received Jane's letter of the 10th Inst with $1.00 Janes letter of the
16th Inst with $2.00 Fathers letter of the 16th Inst with $.50. But I have not
yet heared anything of the Letters that were sent to the Regiment or to
Chambersburg.

I wrote to Capt [James] Starr Last Monday about my Descriptive List,
and also about those letters and I expect an answer from him early next
week. A Descriptive List, gives a Description of the Soldier that it is for. It
gives his hight, collour of hair wiskers. Eyes and Complexion. Also his age.
Ressidence. Where enlisted. When. By whoom sworn into service. &c. It
also gives an account of how much cloathing he has drawn how much he
owes the Government and how much the government owes him. When
Last paid off, Where, and by whoom. If I get my Descriptive List before the
first of November, I can then get mustered for Pay and get Payed off when
the Paymaster comes around to the Hospitals which will probably be a
month later. Or if I have it, I can draw any Cloathing I want, from any
Quarter Master, at any place, and Have it Charged on the Descriptive List.
It is getting too cold now to go out without an Over Coat, and I want to
Draw one as soon as I get my List.

I had an Ague Shake every day last week at 12 o'clock. But have had
none sinse Sunday last. The Rheumatism is pretty bad yet in my shoulders.
Louisa's husband, Mr. Jacobs, gave me something, which I take three
times a Day and I think that is what keeps the Ague off of me.

It is verry dull and Lonesome here in Camp, but I go into town nearly
every Day, so that time Passes verry well. I write my own Passes and
sign the Doctors name to them. I have practiced it so much, that I
dont think the Doctor, could tell the difference himself. It is very cold
here today. The Wind is Blowing a Regular Hurricane, and it is
verry dusty.

I am glad to hear that Fathers head is getting better, he must have
had a severe time of it. The Drafted men are comming in here pretty fast,
those that are able are offering from $300.00 to $600.00 Dollars for
Substitutes and I have known two men who gave a Thousand Dollars

apiece for subs. Give my Love to all the Family. Hoping that you are all well I remain

Your affectionate brother
Tom

Write soon.

Later in October, Smith's mother paid him a visit at the hospital in Harrisburg, although her own health was tenuous. Smith refers to this visit in a letter of October 31 and suggests that the visit to Harrisburg worsened his mother's already delicate health.

Harrisburg Penna
Oct 31st/62

Dear Sister

I received Susans Letter of the 29th Inst last Evening, and was verry glad to hear that Mother got Home safe and well. I was verry much afraid that she would have a sick spell, after her trip up here. You must tell Mother and Susan, that they must not try to have me transferred any more, as I want to stay here a while longer. I think if I stay here, that I can get my Discharge after a while. I have not got my Descriptive List yet, but expect to get it in a few days, when I shall push the Doctors for a Discharge everey day until I get it. Today being the last of the Month, all those who have got their Lists, will be Mustered for Pay and be paid off in a few days. But those who have not got them, will have to wait two months longer.

I am sorry to hear that Bob is in such a bad way. When you write again, give me his Directions, so that I can write to him.

I have no more to say at pressent. Give my love to all the Family. Write soon.

Your affectionate brother
Tom

P.S. Ask Susan what she meens by the Red, White and Black. I do not understand her.

Tom

In his next letter home, Smith poignantly describes the loneliness and
misery that a sick sergeant suffered during his stay at Camp Curtin Hospital.

Harrisburg

Nov 21st/62

Dear Brother

I received your letters of the 14th and 17th Inst. Ever sinse last Satturday,
we have had the most miserable weather, that I have seen for some time.
Cloudy, Foggy, Drisling, and Pouring Rain all the time. Last Sunday I had
a slight touch of the Ague again, and sinse then I have had a Regular
Shake every Day. The Shake comes on me in the Morning Between 10 and
12 o'clock, and lasts from one to one and a half hours. After which I have
a verry high Feever, which lasts from Two to 4 Hours. Then I have slight
Feevers, and Cold Sweats untill midnight. In the mornings I Feel verry
well, but weak untill the Shake comes on me again. I am getting better now
and Expect to be clear of it in two Days more.

I received a Letter from Sergt Finn[20] of our Company last Sunday. He
sent me three Letters, one of them had two Dollars in, but the other two
had nothing. The Letters only got to the Regiment last Wednesday, and he
sent them to me right away. Perhaps the other may turn up yet. One of the
letters was from Jane Dated Sept 15th. One from Susan Dated Oct 3 sent to
the Regiment with two Dollars in it. The other one was from Susan Dated
Oct 7th and Directed to Chambersburg. Our Regiment is at Frederick City
Md. They have verry few Horses, and what they have got are Broken down
and good for nothing. They have received a Large number of Recruits, and
are drilling them.

Louisa gave Birth to a Girl yesterday a week ago, They are getting along
verry well. They send their love to you.

I am verry nervous and cannot hold my Pencil steady any Longer so I
must close. Give my Love to all the Family.

Yours, &c.

Tom

I received the Dollar that Susan sent me in your letter.

Smith refers to the condition of the regiment's horses. After Lee's army
withdrew into Virginia, the Confederate cavalry, commanded by Maj. Gen.

J. E. B. Stuart, went on a raid behind the Union lines. Brig. Gen. John Buford, new chief of cavalry for the Army of the Potomac, sent a large force of Federal cavalry after the Rebel horsemen, including those elements of the Lancers not assigned to Franklin's headquarters. A company of twenty-five men, under the command of Capt. Charles Cadwalader, located the Confederate force and reported its presence to division headquarters.[21]

The rest of the regiment pursued Stuart's horsemen as far as a small Pennsylvania town called Gettysburg. They found the main body of the Rebel cavalry at Emmitsburg, Maryland, about six miles south of Gettysburg, where a large contingent of the regiment was nearly captured. There, on October 11, the Lancers skirmished with Stuart's rear guard as it withdrew into Virginia. Finally, on November 2, Company I was relieved of headquarters duty and returned to the regiment.[22] Smith, however, remained hospitalized in Harrisburg, though he was transferred to a different facility. Again, his loneliness and frustration come through in a letter home written just after Thanksgiving.

East Walnut St. Hospital
Harrisburg Penna
Nov 30th/62

Dear Brother Bennie

I wrote a Letter Home Last week, and have been expecting one from Home all this Week but have not received one yet. Now when you receive this I want you to sit down and write me a great big long Letter and let me know how you all are, and what you are all doing, how is Mother, and is Fathers head got well yet. How did you spend your Thanksgiving Day &c.?

I am in the East Walnut St Hospital now, I came here yesterday a week ago on the 22nd. It is much more comfortable here than what it was out at Camp Curtin, but verry lonesome. The Small Pox is verry bad up here, it broke out in our Hospital last week, we have had seven cases of it, but the Doctors send them off to the Plague House as soon as it showes itself.

The Ladies[23] (God Bless Them) gave us a big Dinner on Thanksgiving Day. We had Turkeys, Geese, Ducks, and Chickens, with Mashed Potatoes, Cold Sloughs, Apple Saus, Cranberry Saus, all kinds of Jelleys and Preserves, Oyster Soup, and Oyster Pie, Cranberry Pie, Minse Pie, Peach Pie, Apple Pie, and Pumpkin Custard, Besides a number of other side dishes too numerous to mention. On Friday we feasted all day off of what was left from Thursdays Dinner. But Bennie do you know that a Crust of Bread and a Glass of Water at Home, would have been much better relished by me, than all the big Dinner that we had here. Well perhaps they will get tired of having me in the Hospital some of these days and Pack me off.

Well I wish they would for it is now nearly Five Months sinse I got sick. I took Sick on the 4th Day of July, and I have only done two Weeks Duty sinse that time. I feel verry well just now. I have not had the Ague sinse Last week.

When you write to Bob give him my Love, and tell him that I would Write to him, but that it is so blame dull up here that I have not got anything to write about. Tell him to write to me and let me know where he is and what they are doing.

The Pay Master has not made his apperence yet, I hope he will come soon as I am getting anxcious to see him, there is a rumer here that he will not come untill after Congress meets, as he has run out of Green Backs and they cannot make any more untill Congress authorises it.

No more at pressent, my Love to you and all the Family. Write soon to. Direct to East Walnut St Hospital Ward No 2

Your affectionate brother

Tom

While Smith remained in the hospital, the Army of the Potomac took to the field again under a new commander, Maj. Gen. Ambrose E. Burnside, who replaced McClellan in mid-November. The Federal host advanced to Fredericksburg, largely unopposed, but found no equipment for bridging the Rappahannock River there, forcing troops to wait for the needed equipment. In the meantime, the Army of Northern Virginia took up a formidable defensive position along high ground to the south and west of the town. The Federal cavalry did not play a major role in this winter campaign, so Smith probably did not miss much by his absence.

The men of the 6th Pennsylvania Cavalry continued to progress as soldiers. After the pursuit of Stuart into Pennsylvania, Company I was relieved from its duty as General Franklin's headquarters guard and rejoined the rest of the regiment as it prepared for the Fredericksburg campaign. After a long march from Washington, the members of Company I arrived in time for the beginning of the battle on December 13.[24] The regiment took no active role in the bloody repulse of Burnside's army.

As his comrades took the field again, Smith stayed in the hospital, where he continued to make sharp and keen observations about Northern society and the plight of the enlisted man in late 1862. Evidence of this may be found in acidic comments made to his sister Jane in the following letter.

Harrisburg
Dec 4th 1862

Dear Sister Jenny

I received Susans Letter of the 28th Ult., and Bennies Letter of the 1st Inst yesterday morning. I am sorry to hear that Susan is in such bad Health, she must take batter care of Herself, or her Health will be entirely ruined after while. I think that she had better give up Teaching School during the Winter, and then by the time that Spring sets in she will be better able to stand it. Tell Susan that one of the Letters that I received from Chambersburg, had a coppy of Bobs first Letter in it. I have not written to Bob yet, for the verry good reason that I have got nothing to write about.

I think that Ben done verry well at the fare, with his Toys and Shels. I hope that whomever has the Reading room and Library in charge, will use some Judgment, and buy Books, and Papers that will be interesting to the Solders, and not ill the shelves with Religeous Books, Sunday School Papers, and Tracts &c. Sometimes wer are half Plagued to Death by members of the upper crust Society (ie) *the Aristockracy*—both Male and Female who fetch such trash as the above to us, and it dont cost them a cent either. We are always glad to see their Backs. I have taken particular notice that all the good things that we get both in the way of Eating and Reading, come from People in the Middle Classes of Society— *Mechanics, Store Keepers* &c—They send us Novels, Historys, Magazine News Papers, &c.

I am sorry to hear that Mother has had another Stroke of the Paulsy. Tell her that she had better give up going to market, and take better care of her Health. She had Ought to keep in the House such bad weather as we have had lately.

When you write again, tell me how the Paulsey opperates when it first comes on, and what are the simptoms afterwords, does it affect the whole boddy or onley parts of it.

Bens Letter was verry good, and I had not trouble at all in Reading it. If he keeps on he will soon beat me at Writing and then I will be the poorest writer in the Familey. Tell him to go to school and studay hard, I expect to hear of him getting in the High School some of these Days. Bye the way, do you and Ben quarle as much as you used to, I hope not, for it is a bad Practice and will grow on you as you get older if you do not break yourselves of it.

You must take good care of your self and not get sick to, for mayby I will want you to nurse me some of these days.

I feel verry well and have a good Appetite, but I have a continual Pain in my Liver and Kidneys which troubles me verry much at times.

I must bring this to a close, for I feel quite Sollemcholy[25] this morning. I always do when I am Writing Home, for it so Lonesome here.

Now hoping that you are a Well and Happy Family,
I am your Sollemcholy

Brother Tom

P.S. I am verry much Oblidged to Mother for sending me that Dollar in Bens Letter for I was broke and it came verry handy.

Tom

As his next letter demonstrates, Smith's illness was not completely incapacitating. We learn that not all of his visits to the home of Cousin Louisa Jacobs and her family were condoned by his doctors. Rather, many of them were the result of a quick trip over the twelve-foot fence surrounding the hospital grounds.

Harrisburg
Dec 10th 1862

Dear Brother

I received your Letter yesterday, and was glad to hear that you are all well at Home.

I am verry well as long as I keep myself quiet, but I cant moove around much.

The Hospitals here were all Paid off the Week before last, except the Camp Curtin Hospital, and I cant get paid untill they do, as I was mustered at Camp Curtin. I went down to see the Pay Master this morning, and he told me that he had no more money, and did not expect to get any before next month. I tell you what I am getting tired of waiting for my money, I hope it will come soon, as I want it.

We have no trouble in getting out of the Hospital (onley a twelve foot fense to climb)—but when we do get out there is nothing to see, nor no place to go to. I think that Harrisburg is the meanest place that I was ever in.

Cos. Louisa and Family are all well; the Baby is getting along fine.

No more at pressent, give my Love to all the Family. Write soon.

Your affectionate brother
Tom

Smith grew deeply depressed with the arrival of the holiday season. His last few letters from Harrisburg reflect a deep sense of despair and an increasing urge to slip the bonds of his hospital tethers. Despite his best efforts to obtain either a furlough home or an outright discharge, he remained a virtual prisoner in the hospital.

Harrisburg
Dec 29th 1862

Dear Sister

I received your Letter of the 20th and Janes of the 26th inst. I am glad that Jane sent me Bobs Letter, it was verry interesting. When you write to Bob again give him my best wishes and tell him he must excuse me for not writing to him, as I have nothing to write about.

I had a shake of the Ague every Day last Week untill Yesterday when it left me. I will not be clear of it again for a few days.

I have tried to get my Discharge but it is no go, the Doctors will not give a Discharge on any Disease there is a possibility of its being cured, unless we have been in the Hospital over Three Months under their charge, so you see there is no chance for me yet, as I have only been here one month, and verry likely I will be sent to some other Hospital before my three months are up.

I have got a verry bad Head Ache and am so nervous that I cannot think of any thing to write about, so I must close. My Love to you and all the Family.

Your affectionate brother
Tom

Write soon

As the year ended, Smith harbored desperate thoughts of slipping away from the hospital without permission and going absent without leave, or taking "French leave," as it was known at the time.

Harrisburg
Jan 7th 1863

Dear Sister

I received yours of the 2nd Inst and am verry sorry to hear that Father is in such bad Health. I suppose that you have got better, as you did not say anything about yourself in your Letter.

I am verry well at pressent. The Ague did not come on my last Sunday as I expected it would, but I guess it will pay me a vissit next Sunday. It always stays away for Seven Fourteen or twenty one Days.

When you write again let me know how Mother is getting along, I hope that her Health is better than what it used to be.

I took Dinner at Cousin Louisa's today. We had a Baked Chicken, Pot Pie and you know I can walk rite into that Dish. Tomorrow I am going up again as they are agoing to have Sower Krout. Bye the way Susan why dont you write to Cossin Louisa? She is always asking affter you and Jane, and I think that it is a downright shame that one of you dont write to her.

Can you read my letters? I do not believe that you can read one half of them as I always scribble them off in such a hurry, just when the notion takes me that I believe that if I was to look over them I could not read them myself.

I must close now as it is getting dark.

My Love to you and all the Family. Write Soon.

Your affectionate brother
Tom

Private

P.S. If you have got two Dollars $2.00 that you do not want to use for a couple of months I wish you would let me have it.

Tom

When you write again let me know if I owe you any more money that what I send you the last time.

Smith's desperation came through in a letter to his brother Joe. The seriousness of his threat to desert grew with the improvement in his health.

Harrisburg

Jan 14th/63

Dear Brother

I received Susans Letter of Jan 11th yesterday morning. I am verry sorry to hear that Father is so sick as to be confined to his Bed. It must go verry hard with him.

I am getting verry harty now, I have not had the Ague for some time, and the Doctor thinks that it will not return again.

I have tried all I know how to get a Furlow but it is no use. I believe if I could get Home for a week or two, that I would be well enough to return to my Regt again.

I seen Charley Penrose and Ben Buck[26] yesterday. They started for home last evening. I think they got quite enough of Harrisburg while here, and I guess they wont want to return again in a hurry.

No more at pressent. My love to all. Write soon.

Your affectionate brother

Tom

Private

Joe I want you to write me a Letter saying that Father is verry sick and not expected to live, that he is anxious to see me and wants me to come Home if only for a few Days. Write a Letter that I can show to the Doctor, and then if he wont give me a Pass to come Home I shall take French. Get enough money from Mother to pay my expenses Home and send it in the Letter.

If I take French I shall send my Baggage by Addams Express Directed to you.

There is a gap in Smith's letters from this letter of January 14, 1863, to April 4, 1863. The medical record log in his pension file indicates that he left the hospital in March. There is no record that he was disciplined for deserting the hospital, but he could have been court-martialed for doing so. Nothing contained in Smith's compiled service records indicates that he ever received the furlough he so desperately wanted.[27] Presumably after five months of recuperation in a place that he clearly despised, Tom Smith was thrilled to leave.

CHAPTER FOUR

"I Have Seen So Much, Heard So Much, and Been So Many Places"

Headquarters Duty during the Chancellorsville Campaign

WHILE SMITH RECUPERATED in the hospital, major changes occurred in the Army of the Potomac. After the Federal repulse at Fredericksburg in December 1862, Burnside tried to redeem himself by launching another campaign, which quickly bogged down in terrible weather and became known as the Mud March. Capt. Emlen N. Carpenter bitterly commented that "the movement so long talked of is over and resulted in nothing. The day we started a storm set in and in a short time the roads became almost impassable. Wagons, ammunition, trains, artillery carriages got stuck fast in the mud. In many case men sank down from sheer exhaustion. Suffering was very great. The pontoons stuck fast—multitudes of horses died. The march seemed what Napoleon's retreat from Moscow might have been."[1]

Burnside recognized that he was not competent to command an army and requested that he be relieved in late January, a request quickly granted by President Lincoln. On January 26, 1863, Maj. Gen. Joseph Hooker, known as "Fighting Joe," was appointed to command the demoralized Army of the Potomac, which went into winter camp on the hills to the north of Fredericksburg.[2]

Hooker immediately set about reforming the army. Among the changes was to organize the cavalry into a single corps of about twelve thousand men, commanded by Maj. Gen. George Stoneman.[3] Three divisions as well as a reserve brigade consisting of the army's Regular cavalry units were created. The Lancers were assigned to independent duty at army headquarters, and on March 1, 1863, Companies E and I were assigned to serve as Hooker's escort. The regiment established a pleasant camp in a stand of pine trees at Belle Plain Landing on the Rappahannock River, where it awaited an assignment.[4]

HeadQuarters Armey of the Potomac Virginia
April 4th 1863

Dear Brother [Joe]

I arrived in Washington last Tuesday at 10 o'clock pm. On Wednesday morning I took the Boat and arrived at Acquia Crick[5] Landing at one o'clock pm and at 3 o'clock pm I took the cars for Falmouth where I arrived safe at 4 o'clock.

Our squadron Companeys I and E are at Genl Hookers Head Quarters about one and half miles from Falmouth. We have got Sibly tents[6] and Sugar Loaf Stoves and are fixed a great Deal more comfortable than what I expected to be.

We are acting as Ordileys and Dispatchers from Gen Hooker and Staff. Gen Hooker is verry well pleased with us, he is getting up a distinct Uniform for us. We are to have corduroy Britches, Light Blue Jacket, Trimed with Red Cord, and a Fancy Cap, also long Cavalry Boots.[7] The day before I got Here our Company turned in all their extra Horses, Armes, and Equipments, so I have got nothing at all to do.

Our Regiment is laying at Bell Plains[8] about 3 miles from here, and I am mighty glad that we are not with them.

The weather has been verry windy sinse I Have been here and the mud is disappering verry fast. When you write let me know what Bregade, Division Bob is in and I will try and get over to see him. Let Bob know whare I am and perhaps he can come and see me.

I sent that velise from Washington, by Addams Express. Let me know when you receive it.

No more at pressent. Write soon. My love to you and all the Family.

Tom

P.S. Has Schwemmer[9] sent for me yet. What did he say. Give my Regard to all the Boys and tell them I am well.

TURN OVER

Have you head from Case yet? Direct your letter to Thomas W. Smith,
General Hookers Head Quarters in care of Capt Starr

The reforms implemented by Hooker showed immediate benefits.
Morale, which had been at an all-time low, began to rise. On March 17, 1863,
the Federal cavalry scored one of its first victories over its Southern counter-
part at the Battle of Kelly's Ford, fought near Culpeper Court House,
Virginia. Then, on April 6, President and Mrs. Lincoln reviewed the entire
Army of the Potomac. While Tom Smith evidently did not appreciate either
the reviews or the president's politics, the reviews worked wonders to restore morale in the ranks of the army, which shook off the lingering effects
of the hardships of winter encampment.

Head Quarters Armey of the Potomac, Virginia
April 10th/63

Dear Joe

I received your Letter Yesterday. When you receive this I wish you would go
to Horstmans 5th and Cherry, and get me a set of sergents Shevrons for the
Sleeves of my Dress Jacket and two yards and three quarters of Sergents
Braid for the Pants (2 3/4 yds—yellow). Let me know how much it costs
and I will send you the money next Pay Day. We are expecting the Pay
Master here every Day, but I will not get anny pay this time as I was not
here on mustering day to get mustered.

Father Linckum, the niggers Father,[10] Wife and Son came down here last
Sunday. Gen Hooker and they have been Reviewing the Armey all this
week, they will return to Washington tomorrow.

I seen John Miller the day before yesterday, I did not get a chance to
speak to him, as we were returning from a Review with Gen Hooker.

We had the same kind of weather last Satturday and Sunday down here
as you had. On Sunday morning there was more snow on the ground than I
have seen this winter, but Sundays rain washed the snow all away, and left
us in a Devil of a mud hole again but we have verry fine weather now and
the mud is Disappering fast. I hope it continues so for I am verry anxcious

to see old Josey make a moove, and when he does look out, for he will eather gain a great Victory, or suffer a great Defeat.

The whole Armey was mustered today and the Rolls will be sent to Washington. Old Abe says he is going to make a Draft and fill up every Regiment to their full standard. Joe I want you to try and get out of the Draft if you can but if you are Drafted try and get into our Company.

No more at pressent. My love to all the Family and all inquiring Friends.

Your brother
Tom

While Smith downplayed the reviews, they were a spectacle. For example, it took more than three hours for the Cavalry Corps to parade past the president. One member of the 8th Illinois Cavalry noted in his journal, "Grand review of the Cavalry. Mud knee deep, but we marched the best we could. Lincoln and his wife were here. The President looks tired but he is as handsome as ever."[11] Maj. Alexander Biddle wrote to his wife, Julia: "the Rush's Lancers are presenting a perfect picture like effect in beautiful order. They side wheeled into line, forming as they came up on the left of the preceding company at a gallop—it was with the Artillery, the most brilliant part of the whole affair. I saw . . . Richard Rush, whom I rode up to be at the head of his regiment on his way home . . ."[12]

The *Philadelphia Inquirer* reported that "the finest cavalry display ever witnessed in the United States, was that of the review of cavalry to-day by the President. Every regiment turned out in its largest possible numbers, and the display was most imposing."[13] As a result of the reforms and the morale boost created by the reviews, the Federal troopers, for the first time, began to believe that they were the equal of the Confederate cavalry.

The grand review also meant that the spring campaigning season was rapidly approaching. Hooker developed a plan to steal a march around Lee's flank near a crossroads called Chancellorsville, located in a tangled, dense forest of undergrowth known as The Wilderness. To create a diversion, Hooker sent the Cavalry Corps, save for one division, on a far-ranging raid on Richmond, leaving his army largely unscreened. The cavalry was to cut Lee's lines of communications with Richmond and destroy, to the extent possible, the Aquia and Richmond Railroad. The Cavalry Corps began its movement on April 13, 1863. However, torrential rains flooded the Rappahannock River and delayed the beginning of the great raid until April 29.[14]

Head Quarters Armey of the Potomac
April 16th 1863

Dear Brother

I received your Letter and the Striping yesterday. I am glad to hear that
Mother is getting better and that the rest of the Family are all well.

My Health is verry good, but my Back is verry weak and pains me verry
much at times.

Last Satturday there was a Swiss General[15] come down here to vissit
the troops, and on Sonday myself and ten men were out with him to Review
the 5th Armey Corps. After we got through with them we went to Review
the Cavalry, but found that they were all packing up to moove. We then
Returned to Head Quarters. On Monday Morning the Cavelry and Light
Artillery commensed to moove.[16] It was given out that the Rebs Had made
another Raid into Maryland and Pennsylvania, and that our boys were
marching to cut off their retreat, but I think that was a Blind to Close the
Eyes of Spies.

On Tuesday Several of our Boys were sent with Dispatches to Gen
Stoneman at Kelleys Ford 25 miles above this and when they returned they
said that there was considerable fighting going on up there and that our
Boys were trying to cross the Rapahanock.[17] We also hear that they (our
troops) are trying to cross near the King Georges Inn 20 miles below this
Point. We have used up 5 Horses sinse Monday carrying Dispatches to the
Above named Places. Our men are kept going night and day, always the
same order (Dont spare your Horse). On Tuesday night it commensed to
Rain and Poured down Incessently all night all Day yesterday and all night
Last night. Today it has been clear, but it is now beginning to Rain again
and it Looks as though it would continue for some time. The boys are
afraid that there will another mud Skedaddle, but I think that the Troops
will stay whare they are untill the weather is cleared off again.

If it had not been for this Rain I have doubt but there would have been
a General Engagement all along our Lines by this time.

Bob got your Letter on Monday night and on Tuesday morning he came
over to see me, he looks verry well. He told me that he expected to get his
Furlough in a few Days. But I do not think he will get it yet awhile for
Hooker has Ordered them to be stopped for the Pressent.

Those Shevrons that you sent me are too Large and they have got
Quartermasters Braid on them. I wish you would try and get them

exchanged for a set with narrower Braid on them. If you cannot get them exchanged send me two yards and a half (2 $^1/_2$ yards) of Plain Braid Like Sample, or Plain Corded Braid. Send me a skein of Black Thread and a skein of yellow sewing silk. I do not like to put you to so much trouble but I cannot help myself down here. Let me know how much it costs.

No more at pressent. My Love to all the Family.

Your brother
Tom

You can eather get the Braid Like Sample or a size between the two.

Smith's guess about the imminence of a general engagement was accurate. Hooker planned to move his gigantic 133,000-man army on April 27. The preparations for his grand advance are well noted in Smith's letter of April 24.

Head Quarters Armey of the Potomac, Virginia
April 24th/63

Dear Brother

I received your Letter Yesterday. Those Chevrons are the verry thing, they are the neatest set that I have yet seen, when you write again let me know how much they cost and I will send you the monney.

I went over to see Bob last Monday. It commensed to Rain when I got over to his camp, they were out on Picket but I waited untill they came in, it was Raining verry hard and Bob was wet through so I did not stay long. Bob is well. The Corn Exchange have a verry nice Camp and good Quarters. All the Infantry have got 5 Days Rations in their Knap Sacks and three Days in their Haver Sacks. They have been under marching Orders ever sinse the Cavelry mooved up the River. Four times within the last two weeks we have been on the Eve of mooving, but every time we have been disappointed by the Weather. The night before last we were expecting to moove at every moment, but at 9 pm it commensed to Rain, and Rained all night, all Day yesterday, and all night Last night. This morning it was clear and the Sun was out, but now (10 am) it is Raining like the Devil again. A man from our Company, Joe Dougherty went Home on a Furlough a few Days ago, I sent my Carpet Bag home with him. I was agoing to get you to send some things on with Him for me, but I guess you had better not send them, as I am afraid that he does not intend to return.[18]

I sent Fourty Dollars to you by Addams Express. Give Mother Thirty Dollars Susan Five Dollars and yourself Five Dollars. Four Dollars that I borrowed from you, and One Dollar for that first set of Chevrons. Let me know if your own and Susans account is right, for my memmory is so bad that I am afraid that I have made a Mistake.

Enclosed I send you Fifty Cents. Pay the Express bill. If it costs more than that, Let me know.

Whenever there is anything Particular in the Papers you may send them if you will. It is reported here that the Cavalry succeded in crossing the Rapahanock at Kelleys Ford the Day before Yesterday. If it is true they will be verry apt to catch the Devel, as this Rain has raised the River so much, that they will not be able to recross, and we will not be able to reenforse them.[19]

I had intended to send Home Fifty Dollars, but my Boots are played out and I must have a new Pair. The Sutlers here have two kinds of Boots, one kind they ask 11.00 Dollars for and the other kind 15.00 Dollars and neather of them are worth a cus. Have you ever received that carpet bag with the cloathing in that

[the balance of this letter is missing]

The infantry began moving on April 27, and the men were optimistic about the prospects for the campaign. The bulk of the army crossed the river at Kelly's Ford. Meanwhile, two corps were detached and sent across at Fredericksburg. Their mission was to capture Marye's Heights, above the town, and to keep the Confederate forces there pinned down, preventing them from being shifted to meet Hooker's main force. Pontoon bridges were pushed to the river, and the Union infantry poured into the already devastated town of Fredericksburg.

Head Quarters Armey of the Potomac
Wednsday April 29th 1863

Dear Brother

On Sunday and Monday the Weather was clear, Dry, and Windy, and by Monday Evening the Mud was all Dryed up, and the Roads were in splendid condition for marching. On Monday Evening we got Orders from

Gen Hooker to have twenty of the best Men and Horses with 5 Days Rations ready to go with him at a moments Notice. Early on Tuesday morning they started up the River, and soon after they started it commensed to Rain again. But the whole Armey was on the moove, had been mooving all night and it was now too late to stop. The 1st 3rd and 6th Corps mooved down to whare Franklins Grand Division crossed at the battle of Fredericksburg, which is about one mile below the City of and just oppisite to where we are. On Tuesday night the Fog was so thick that you could not see a Brick House 10 yds off. During the night the Infantry carried the Pontoon Boats down to the waters edge and just before Daylight they shoved them into the water, filled them with men, and pusshed off boldly for Rebbeldom. They were received by the Rebs with volleys of musketry, but succeded in Landing drove the Rebs back and took about two hundred Prissoners. They then went to work Lively, and in a short time Had two Pontoon Bridges Layed across the River, and our Troops crossed over.

Everything was arranged so well and conducted so quietly, that men who were Laying down a few yds from the waters edge did not know that our troops had attempted to cross untill they were Fired on by the Rebs.

Gen Hooker returned to Head Quarters at noon today. He Had been up as far as Kelleys Ford. Our Boys say that the 11th and 12th Corps were crossing at Kelleys Ford, also that Stonemans Cavalry which is the 8th Corps.[20] There was considerable skirmishing and Artillery Firing going on there when they left. It has Cleared off this Evening. The moon and Stars are shining brightly. I expect to hear Revellee sounded from the Cannons mouth in the morning.

I received your Letter, and Postage Stamps this evening. The Carpet Bag that I sent with Dougherty was empty. When you write again let me know if you received the Carpet Bag that I sent from Washington with the cloathing in it.

Thursday April 30th 10 am

It commensed to Rain about the middle of the night and still continues. I begin to think that the clerk of the wether must be on the side of the Rebs, for he opposes us in every moove we make.

Two of our men carried dispatches up to United States Ford[21] last night, and returned this morning. They say that Couch 2nd Corps, and Meads 5th Corps, were attempting to cross there during the night. United States Ford is about Half Way between this and Kelleys Ford.

Some of our Troops are crossing at Banks Ford about 8 mile below here, and some still further down, but I cannot learn what Corps they are. Had the wether been clear today, I have no Doubt that the Battle wold have commensed in earnest this morning. But I am afraid that this Rain will knock the Devil out of Hookers plans. However the Battle has got to be Fought anyhow, for we have gone too far to fall back now.

No more at pressent. My Love to all the Family, and all inquiring Friends. Hoping that you are all well I remain your

Affectionate brother
Tom

On April 30, the optimistic Hooker issued a General Order to the army that would prove hollow: "It is with heartfelt satisfaction the commanding general announces to the army that the operations of the last three days have determined that our enemy must ingloriously fly, or come out from behind his defenses and give us battle on our own ground, where certain destruction awaits him."[22] Only the part about the Confederates coming out from behind their defenses proved true.

Once again, Tom Smith was correct in his predictions. The Battle of Chancellorsville was fought on May 1–4, 1863. Despite the fact that he had stolen a march on Lee as well as his great numerical advantage, Hooker lost the fight badly. After a day of fighting on May 1, Hooker pulled back into a defensive posture, announcing to Maj. Gen. Darius N. Couch, commander of the Second Corps, that he had "Lee just where I want him; he must fight me on my own ground." Couch later wrote, "The retrograde movement had prepared me for something of the kind, but to hear from his own lips that the advantages gained by the successful marches of his lieutenants were to culminate in fighting a defensive battle in that nest of thickets was too much, and I retired from his presence with the belief that my commanding general was a whipped man."[23]

On the morning of May 2, Stuart discovered that the Federal right was "in the air"; the withdrawal of the Federal cavalry for the great raid left inadequate mounted support to protect Hooker's flanks. Capitalizing on the opportunity, Lee ordered Jackson to march around Hooker's right and strike the exposed flank. Jackson succeeded in surprising the Union Eleventh Corps, made up mostly of German immigrants, while its men were cooking their dinners in the late afternoon. A rout ensued, and only a spirited stand by Couch's Second Corps at a place called Hazel Grove saved Hooker's army from annihilation. While carrying dispatches from army headquarters to the front lines, Smith witnessed the severe fighting at Hazel Grove.

Head Quarters Armey of the Potomac Virginia
May 8th/63

Dear Brother

The Armey of the Potomac has Fought another great Battle and been defeated, as you have probably heard through the papers, before this reaches you. I have seen so much, heard so much, and been so many places, that I do not know what to write about. However, I will try and give you some of my experiense on the Battle Field.

Last Thursday (April 30th) at Four O'Clock pm, Gen. Hooker gave us Orders for 40 men to go with him as Escort. We went up to United States Ford and crossed the River, and then mooved on to Chancellorsvill, which place we reached about 11 o'clock pm. On Friday there was skirmishing all day along our lines, and a Pretty Heavy Battle on our Left. Our Left drove the Rebs about 1 mile during the Day but had to fall back again toward Evening to their first Position.[24]

On Satturday the Enemy made several attempts to fors our Center but were Repulsed every time.[25] Towards evening they attacked our Right in Forse and here the most disgraseful Rout occured that I have ever heard tell of. The 11th Corps Broke and Ran away, Fled, Skedaddled like a Flock of Sheep. Throwing knapsacks, guns, ammunition, and everything thay had away. I saw the Rebs with my own Eyes throw down their Guns, and run after the damn Dutchmen catch them by the Back of their necks and take them Prisoners. This is Seigles old Command, now commanded by Gen. Howard (I Fights mit Seigle).[26] But the 2nd Corps (Gen Couch) came up in fine style, at a Double Quick, and soon Regained the ground that the 11th had lost. This Fight lasted well into the Night and the Rebs must have suffered terrably in killed and Wounded from our Artillery.[27]

On Sunday morning the Rebs attacked us all along our lines. Our Left during the night had thrown up Brestworks, and held their own Bravely. But our Right gradually fell back, Desperately contesting every Inch of the ground as they went, untill our Left Center had to fall back with them to keep our Lines connected. During all this time our Left, and Left Center were under a galling cross Fire from the Rebble Artillery. Our Reserves were not idle, they were buisily engaged throwing up entrenchments, and about the middle of the day our lines fell back onto them.

Here again the Enemy made several desperate attempts to forse our Center by charging en mass, driving our Skirmishers and Infantry into the Entrenchments. But Each and every time they were terrably Repulsed by the Grape and Cannister of our Artillery. Throughout Monday, and Tuesday, the Battle was carried on in the same style, the Enemy attacking our Entrenchments and being Repulsed every time.[28]

On Tuesday Afternoon it commensed to Rain, and I never seen it Rain harder in my life. In the Evening Gen Hooker sent in a Flag of Truse and soon after Dark we commensed to moove down to United States Ford and recross the River. We had three Pontoon Bridges down, but the Water Raised so high, that we had to take one of them up to lengthen out the other two. On Wednesday we returned to our old Head Quarters near Falmouth.

Gen Hooker was always in the thickest of the Fight, and while the Fight was going on his head Quarters was in the saddle, at other times it was always on the Front. Once we thought we had lost him, he was struck in the Brest by a splinter of a Post, and knocked to the Ground but was soon in the saddle again.[29] We had two men slightly wounded, one on the hand by a Piece of Shell and the other in the side by a peise of shell. Our Buglers horse was struck by a shell and killed under Him. Captain Starr had one Horse killed by a Rifle Ball. On Sonday I took a Dispatch to Gen Couch. He was standing on the brestworks while I was waiting for an Answer the Rebs made a charge en mass on our lines, they came up 25 or 30 Deep yelling like Hyeneas. Our Artillery poured in the Grape and Cannister mowing them down by Hundreds. Still they closed up and came on, they were within 50 yds of us, I thought it was all up, but no, Couch was prepared for them, he had Artillery in the Edge of the Woods which I did not see, now they open on them. Our Infantry Ralley on the Entrenchments and pour a deadly volley of musketry right into the Enemys fase, their yell ceases, they waver, break and Run, The our Boys gave three times three cheers that would have done your heart good to hear. All this took plase in a good deal less time than it takes me to write it.

The Day when I opened the bundle on the back of my Saddle I found a Rifle Ball lodged in my Paper and Envelops. My Horse was wounded slightly in the Leg by a Piese of shell, but not disabled, and I received a ball through my canteen.

I saw Bob last Sunday on the Battle Field. He had not been to the Front yet but expected to go in next. I hope that he has got through as safe as I have.

Gen Hallack[30] and Old Abe came down here yesterday morning and Returned to Washington last Night.

At the time that the Battle was going on at Chancellorsvill, Gen Sedgewick[31] crossed the River at Frecericksburg and took the Hights[32] on the other side. But the Rebs Received Reenforsements from Richmond and drove Sedgewick back again. I do not know what Hooker Retreated for. For we could have held our position and entrenchments against any numbers that the Enemy could have brought to bare against us.

I think that Hooker will cross again in a short time. And if he does this Armey will get wipped so damn bad that they wont know themselves. I never seen the Armey so much demorralised as it is at the Pressent time. However the men do not blame Hooker for he done all that was in the power of man to do. I think that the Enemey have lost two men to our one in killed and wounded, for they were the attacking party. But they have taken a great many more Prissoners than we have.

The rain still continues.

I have not seen a newspaper for 10 Days, except the Sunday Transcript that you sent me.

I am well except my Back, it Pains me so much that I have not been out of my tent sinse I came back. My Love to all the Family. Write soon.

Yours &c.

Tom

Chancellorsville cost Robert E. Lee Stonewall Jackson. Jackson was out scouting for an opportunity to attack Hooker when he was mortally wounded by his own men in a confused sequence of events. Despite the loss, Chancellorsville proved victorious for the Confederates. The Federals sustained more than seventeen thousand casualties in the battle, the Confederates nearly thirteen thousand.[33] Yet another defeat demoralized the Federals, as reflected in Smith's letters home.

In losing the battle, Hooker conceded the initiative to Lee. Pvt. Clement Hoffman of Company E, also assigned to headquarters escort duty, wrote home to his mother: "Gen'l Hooker is a bold and fighting Gen'l, but not one to plan out maneuvering of a large Army. . . ."[34]

Head Quarters Armey of the Potomac
May 22ⁿᵈ 1863

Dear Brother [Joe]

Your own and Susan Letters came to Hand in due time were gladly Received
as Letters from Home always are.

I have not been verry well for the last Week. I am afraid it will go with
me as it did last Summer. I have got continued Pain in my Bowels and
Head Ache all the time, and always feel like vomiting. My appetite is
completely gone.

Capt Starr has gone Home for a few Days and if the Prayers of
this Squadron were answered he would not Return again. He has acted
like a Perfect Tyrent sinse we returned from across the River. But I
will give you more particulars some other Time when I feel better than I
do today.

I do not think that this Armey can moove for some time yet as Head
Quarters were mooved the other day about 1 mile from the old Place into
the Woods.

After the late Battle was fought all News Papers were stopped from
coming into this Armey. The first Paper that I saw after the Battle was the
Transcript and Press that you sent me wraped up together. But they come
more regularly now all except the New York Herrald which is not allowed to
come into the Armey.

I wish you would send me a box of Blue Pecippet or Blue Ointment, you
can send it by mail.

No more at Pressent. My Love to all the Family. Hoping that you all are
well I remain

Your affectionate brother
Tom

Enclosed I send you One Dollar to Pay for the Ointment. If it costs less
than that send me the Ballance in Postage Stamps.

Hooker blamed reporters for his loss and banned them and their papers
from the army's camps. Doubtless, this did little to restore the men's
morale. As Hooker sat, Lee decided to invade the North. The Rebel army
massed near Culpeper Court House, and all of the Confederate cavalry concentrated there while it prepared to cover Lee's main force.

Head Quarters Armey of the Potomac
June 2nd/63

Dear Brother

I received your Letter last week. Also the Box of Ointment. I am glad to hear that you are all well at Home. I have got right well again.

Last Friday I went to see Bob, but his Division had broke camp early in the Morning and mooved somewhere up the River, so I did not get to see him. When he writes Home I wish you would let me know where he has mooved to.

It is verry dusty and disagreeable down here, we have had no Rain sinse we returned from up the River.

Col. Rush has left our Regiment. He is appointed to the command of the Invalid Corps at Washington.[35]

The Regiment have turned in their Lances and ordered Carbines.[36] I am in hopes that we will turn in our Lances in a few days. No more at pressent. Write soon. Hoping that you are all as well as I am, I remain

Your affectionate brother
Tom

P.S. What do the Market Compy. Intend to Build on Twelfth Street. If you get $7000 for the House, what do you intend to do with the Money.

Stoneman's weary troopers finally rejoined the Army of the Potomac on May 16 after two grueling weeks in the saddle. The balance of the Lancers marched with Brig. Gen. John Buford's reserve brigade, made up of the Regular cavalry units attached to the Army of the Potomac. During the long raid, the men of the 6th saw difficult service and earned the respect of their hard-bitten brigade commander. In his after-action report, Buford noted, "The 6th Pennsylvania Cavalry, under Major Morris, had its equal share of trials and exposure, and has been more than equal to any task imposed on it." Sgt. Christian Geisel of Company H wrote that "From the 29th of April to the 9th of May we only had our horses unsaddled about three hours, after the provisions had run out we carried along we lived on ham and corncakes of which we found a large quantity stored away in some places."[37] After its fine performance during Stoneman's Raid, the regiment was permanently attached to the reserve brigade, but Smith's Company I remained on escort duty with army headquarters.

Richard Rush's tenure as a regimental commander ended quietly. On April 25, he wrote, "I am mortified that . . . I have not the physical endurance to retain my health under the vicissitudes of our cavalry campaign." His cousin Julia's husband, Maj. Alexander Biddle of the 121st Pennsylvania Volunteer Infantry, wrote, "Richard Rush is looked upon as almost not of the Army. He has a desk in the War Department, as Chief of the Invalid Corps and will probably never rejoin his regiment. I think he has ruined his military career."[38] However, the regiment Rush formed would bear his name for the rest of its existence.

Tom Smith wrote home on June 8, not knowing that the Confederate invasion of the North was scheduled to begin the next day. In his letter he professes a vague sense of unease that permeated the Army of the Potomac as Hooker attempted to figure out what Lee's next move would be.

> Head Quarters Armey of the Potomac
> June 8th/63

Dear Brother

I Received Jenny's Letter a few days ago, and I am verry sorry to hear that Mother and Susan are sick. I hope that when this reaches Home they will be well again. You must tell the rest of the Family that they must not be offended because I do not write to them, for when I write to one I intend it for all.

For the last 8 or 10 Days the Rebs have been mooving on the other side of the River, but there are so many rumors about them that we do not know what to believe. Some say that they intend crossing above somewhere and others say that they are marching against Keys on the Peninsula. Others again think that they have sent the bulk of their Forses away to Reinforse other Points, and are threatening our Front to keep us from attacking them.

On Friday the 5th Inst we laid a Pontoon Bridge below Fredericksburg, and threw a bregade of our forses across the River, there was some verry heavy cannonading. Today I hear that our Forses are Recrossing and Taking up the Pontoons

June 9th a.m. It is false that our Troops have Recrossed again. We have one Division of the 1st Corps, and one Division of the 6th Corps on the other side of the River. They are throwing up heavy Entrenchments.

We had an artist here the other Day, who took a Photograph of our Company first mounted and then dismounted. Perhaps you will see them in Philadelphia, if you let me know if you can Recognize me on them. My Helth is good. No more at Pressent. Give my Love to all the Family.

Your Brother

Tom

P.S. I wish you would send Five Dollars $5.00 in your next, you can get it from Mother.

Have you ever seen Bill Turner or Carter sinse I left Home. How are all the Boys and what are they doing. Have you got the Books yet.

Tom

As Tom Smith indicated, the Union Cavalry Corps crossed the Rappahannock River at Beverly's and Kelly's Fords and struck the entire force of Confederate cavalry at Brandy Station. Nearly twenty-one thousand mounted troopers were involved, making it the largest all-cavalry engagement ever fought in North America. It also marked the opening of the Gettysburg campaign.

CHAPTER FIVE

"The Sixth Pennsylvania Never Runs!"

Fighting with the Army of the Potomac—
Gettysburg and After

FOLLOWING A SERIES of meetings held in Richmond, the Confederate leadership decided to again invade the North, this time to relieve pressure on the beleaguered Southern garrison at Vicksburg and to give the war-weary people of Virginia a respite from the ravages of war. Lee also wanted to lure Hooker's army out into the open, where he could destroy it.

Accordingly, the Army of Northern Virginia began concentrating in the Culpeper County, Virginia, area. J. E. B. Stuart called all of the far-flung elements of his cavalry command together near the town of Culpeper Court House, where he held several grand reviews of his nine thousand cavalrymen. Lee ordered his command to march north on June 9, with Stuart's cavalry leading the way.[1] Union intelligence quickly spotted the concentration of Rebel cavalry, and Hooker responded by ordering a large force of Union cavalry, including the Lancers, to the area to watch the Confederates.[2] By this time, the Lancers had formally joined the Reserve Brigade, serving with the First, Second, Fifth, and Sixth U.S. Cavalry regiments.

Hooker ordered Brig. Gen. Alfred Pleasonton, new commander of the Army of the Potomac's Cavalry Corps, to take his command, fall upon the Confederate cavalry force, and disperse it.[3] Two columns of Yankee cavalry would attack Stuart's force, thought to be concentrated at Culpeper Court House. The northern prong, the Army of the Potomac's First Cavalry Division, along with fifteen hundred select infantry commanded by Brig. Gen. John Buford, would cross the Rappahannock River at Beverly's Ford and advance to Culpeper. The southern column, commanded by Brig. Gen. David M. Gregg and consisting of the Second and Third Divisions of the

Cavalry Corps and another fifteen hundred select infantry, would cross at Kelly's Ford and attack Stuart from the southern approach.

This plan was based on faulty intelligence. Rather than being concentrated at Culpeper, the Confederate force lay just across the Rappahannock, and Buford's opening attack immediately encountered stiff resistance just on the other side of the river. Surprised by the unexpected opposition, Buford's advance quickly bogged down near a place called St. James Church, where Stuart's horse artillery was concentrated.

In response, Buford ordered the Lancers to charge across a field about eight hundred yards wide under heavy artillery fire. The Lancers made a "dash of conspicuous gallantry" across the field and into the teeth of the Southern artillery. The Pennsylvanians "charged the enemy home, riding almost up to the mouths of [the] cannon," nearly capturing two of the Confederate guns.[4] Maj. Robert Morris, Jr., commanding the regiment, was captured when his horse failed to clear a ditch and fell in the path of the charge. One of the Rebel gunners recalled, "Never rode troopers more gallantly . . . , as under a fire of shell and shrapnel, and finally of cannister, they dashed up to the very muzzles, then through and beyond our guns." Major Whelan reported, "The Rebel cavalry, being greatly superior in number to us, closed in on [our] front and both flanks, thus completely surrounding us."[5] Seeing the predicament of the Lancers, Buford ordered the Sixth U.S. Cavalry to their support. Together, the two regiments cut their way out and escaped across the field.

Later that day, Buford again ordered the Lancers to make a mounted charge across an open field of fire. Maj. Henry C. Whelan, who took command of the regiment after Morris's capture, had his horse "Lancer" shot out from under him. Whelan wrote that the second charge was "decidedly the hottest place I was ever in. A man could not show his head or a finger without a hundred rifle shots whistling about. . . . The air [was] almost solid with lead."[6] Late in the afternoon, the Union cavalry withdrew. The battle was a tactical draw and left Stuart's command intact.

With only five companies of Lancers engaged in the fight that day, the regiment sustained the second highest number of casualties of any Union regiment, losing many of its officers. Major Morris was captured, and Capt. Charles B. Davis was killed. Sgt. Lewis Miller of Company L lamented that the loss of Morris "was worse than one hundred men." Capt. Charles Leiper and Lt. Rudolph Ellis were both wounded.[7] Lts. Thompson Lennig and Samuel R. Colladay were reported missing. Eight of the officers had their horses shot out from under them. Major Whelan noted, "The conduct of the officers and men of the regiment was so uniformly good that it is impossible to mention any for particular distinction." Maj. Charles J. Whiting, commander of the Reserve Brigade, praised the Lancers: "No old regiment could have conducted itself better."[8]

Buford noted that the 6th Pennsylvania "covered itself with glory" at Brandy Station. The next day, Buford told Pleasonton, "These men did splendidly yesterday. I call them now my Seventh Regulars."[9] Several days later, Pvt. Clement Hoffman of Company E wrote home to his mother somewhat bitterly: "we have always went by the name of Rushes Lancers, but we are known now to be the 6th Pa. Cavalry for we have turned in our lances we have carried them going on two years and have never had a chance to make a charge with them to any advantage . . . our regiment was the first to charge on the rebels and were pretty well cut up when if they had had their lances when they charged they would have not been half so much cut up, but however as it was they gave the rebels a pretty good rub."[10]

The battering at Brandy Station put the Lancers out of action for several weeks, during which they rested and refit. Tom Smith briefly described the battle to his brother Joe.

Dumfries
June 15th 1863

Dear Brother

I received your Letter last Friday. I have tried to find out where Bob is but I cannot do so, the Armey has been mooving for the Last two weeks, and the 5th Corps are scattered all over the Armey.

Head Quarters mooved yesterday, we marched to Dumfries by way of Stafford Court House. We will moove on again this morning. Gen Hooker keeps his own counsel well, his own staff officers do not know what is going on, but it is Generally believed that we are falling back to Washington. Five Companeys of our Regiment were in that Fight at Kelleys Ford. Capt Dalgrean one of Gen Hookers staff officers, and a Capt in the 2nd United States Regular Cavalry says that he never seen men Fight so well in his Life.[11] He says that when they charged and had their Horse Disabled they took to Bushwacking and Fought with the Infantry with their Carbines. Major Morris led our men to the Charge and when they were serrounded and Morris fell, it was Capt Dalgrean who rallied our men on

their Collors, and Charging the Enemey cut their way out again.[12] The
Bugle is sounding Saddle up.

Tom

Unfortunately, the great cavalry battle only delayed Lee's invasion by a
day. On June 10, Confederate infantry began moving north, with the Union
army following. By June 15, the Reserve Brigade reached Thoroughfare Gap
and had a brief skirmish when troopers of the 6th Pennsylvania found Rebel
troops picketing the entrance to nearby Manassas Gap, providing evidence that the Southern army was concentrating in the Loudoun Valley of
Virginia.[13] A series of cavalry engagements between Stuart's command,
trying to screen Lee's advance, and the Federal cavalry occurred at Aldie,
Middleburg, and Upperville on June 17, 19, and 21, respectively. The battered Lancers sat out these fights at Fairfax Station, missing some of the
finest cavalry fighting of the war.

The Army of the Potomac cautiously followed Lee's advance. Hooker
desperately sought further information regarding the whereabouts of the
Confederate army. Native Pennsylvanians like the Lancers grew worried as
Lee's army entered the Keystone State. Clement Hoffman wrote home, "I
am perfectly satisfied being whare I am for we have a chance of seeing and
knowing all of the movements which this Army makes, I am well satisfied
with the duty which we perform and could not wish for anything beter."[14]
Smith agreed.

Poolesville Maryland
Satturday June 27th/63

Dear Sister

You Folks at Home must excuse me for not writing sooner, but the fact is
for the last two weeks we have been kept so buissy, that it seems more like
an indistinct Dream to me than anything else. We have been kept running
Night and Day ever sinse we left the Rapahanock. I received Joe's Letter last
week, and Jenny's interesting Letter this week. If the Rebs are marching
through the old Keystone State I think they will get into a Trap.[15] For if the
Malitia are able to hold them in check at Harrisburgh,[16] and Hookers
Armey in their Rear which it is by this time or will be in a few Hours! We
have got them Foul.

When I last wrote Home last Monday [June 15] a week we were at
Dumfries we marched that Day to Fairfax Station.

Sunday June 28th Frederick City

I was Interrupted yesterday morning by orders to march. I will now com-
mense again where I left off.

We layed at Fairfax Station untill Wednesday Afternoon [June 24], when
we marched to Fairfax Court House. We Layed at Fairfax Court House untill
the day before yesterday morning when we marched to Poolesville Md. We
crossed the Potomac at Edwards Ferry on Pontoon Bridges. Yesterday
morning we marched to Frederick City.

On Thursday Night I carried Dispatches from Fairfax Court House
to Aldie a distance of 48 miles in 8 hours and as soon as I returned at
3 o'clock a.m. I started on that march to Poolesville 35 miles. My hours
Dropped Dead soon after I got to Poolesville. So yesterday I had to walk to
this Place, I did not get here untill 7 o'clock p.m.

I think Hooker will make this his Head Quarters for a few Days at Least.
I expect to get another Hoarse today.

No more at pressent. Hoping that you are all well I am

Your affectionate brother
Tom

Write soon

Private

P.S. If you have got Five Dollars that you do not want to use at Pressent I
wish you would lend it to me untill Pay Day.

Tom

Tell Joe he must write to me often and let me know his Adventures as a
Soldier, and tell me if any of the rest of the Boys have gone.

Smith later sent home what might have been a portion or transcript
of a diary that contains a detailed description of his whereabouts and
activities during this period. He also described the Battle of Gettysburg.
Smith failed to record in his narrative that Hooker was relieved at his own
request on June 28 and was replaced by another Philadelphian, Maj. Gen.

George Gordon Meade, formerly commander of the Fifth Corps. Clement Hoffman noted, "It is my opinion that the President had relieved [Hooker] for fear that he would get outgeneralled again as he was at Chancellorsville."[17]

Frederick City Md.
June 28th 1863

Wrote a letter to Susan. Layed at this place all Day, got a New Hoarse. On the 29th marched to Middleburg Md and Layed there untill 30th and marched to Tawneytown Md.[18] Layed at Tawneytown untill 10 o'clock p.m. July 1st and marched to the Front near Gettysburg Pa.[19] On July 2nd there was Heavy Skirmishing all Day with Artillery Firing on our side, which the Rebs did not answer untill $4^{1}/2$ o'clock p.m. When the Engagement became general all along out lines. They pressed our Left verry hard untill $7^{1}/2$ p.m. when we repulsed them.[20] At mid day July 2nd our Lines were in the same position as in the Morning but our Skirmishers were some what advanced.

Friday July 3rd. They engaged our Right pretty hard all the morning[21] but at the same time they were massing their Forsses on our left. At 1 o'clock p.m. the Rebs opened a terable fire on our Left and Center from 16 Batteries. They tried verry hard to break our left. Charging by whole Divisions but after a severe contest were hand somely repulsed. Gen Longstreet charged in person at the Head of his Division on our Left.[22]

Satturday 4th, Sunday 5th and Monday 6th, we stayed at the same Place that is Head Quarters near Gettysburg. On Tuesday 7th, we marched to Frederick City Md. On Wednesday 8th marched to Middletown. On Thursday 9th marched to within 2 miles of Boonsborough and Encamped in the Mountains.[23] On Friday 10th marched at 3 o'clock a.m. 4 miles beyond Boonesborough and Encamped on Antietam Creek.

Clement Hoffman, whose Company E was with Smith's Company I at Meade's headquarters on July 3, wrote: "about noon the Rebels opened on our left & center with all of the artillery they had in the intention of breaking our lines, but they found it a mistake. . . . it was the hardest Artillery fighting that ever took place during this war; . . . I was at the front during all of the fight and came safe and sound altho both men and a wonderful sight of horses fell all around me. . . . our captain had both of his horses shot dead and slightly wounded himself some half a dozen of our company had their horses shot but no one was killed."[24] Because the two companies served together, Smith's experience probably was very similar to Hoffman's.

After Gettysburg, the two foes stayed on the field, licking their wounds. On the fifth, Lee began his retreat to Virginia amid torrential rains, with Meade cautiously following. Finding a few free moments on July 11, Smith penned a wonderfully descriptive letter about the climax of the battle to his sister Susan.

> Head Quarters Armey of the Potomac Md.
> July 11th 1863
>
> Dear Sister
>
> Sinse I last Wrote Home the Armey of the Potomac has had some verry hard Fighting but I suppose you Folks at Home know more about it than I doo. I have only seen two News Boys in the last two weeks and they had nothing but the Baltimore Clipper and it had nothing of any account in it.
>
> At the Battle of Gettysburg Gen Mead had his Head Quarters at a White Frame House 50 yds in Rear of the Left Center.[25] The Staff Officers and Orderlies were all in the Garden around the House (a space of about 30 yds square). At this point our Lines took a turn to the Right so that Head Quarters were under a terrable Cross Fire from the Rebble Artillery. There were 21 Horses killed outright in the Garden at Head Quarters. We Lost 11 Horses out of our Sqaddron, Capt Carpenter[26] of Comp E lost two Horses.
>
> Nearly every Horse at Head Quarters was wounded or scrached by pieces of Flying Shell, some of them so bad that they had to be Killed afterwards. There were several Officers and men killed, and some badly Wounded at Head Quarters, but strange to say Comp I had not one man disabled, though several of them were struck by Pieces of Shell.
>
> We gained a great Victory and took Thoussands of Prissoners. In fact the Prissoners came in in such droves that at one time they created a slight pannick in our Reserve who thought that the Rebs had forsed our Line of Battle. We are expecting another Battle now every Hour (8 o'clock a.m.) We are all saddled up and expect the General to go to the Front every moment.[27]
>
> I Received Father's Letter of the 3rd Inst. Tell Mother that I received the 5 Dollars that she sent me at Fairfax Station Virginia.

I seen Bobs Regt at Middletown the Day before Yesterday. I inquired for him but he was in the Rear with the Waggon Train so I did not get to see him.

My helth was never better than it is now. I have felt so well and Hardy for the Last month that I begin to think that I was never in good Helth before.[28]

No more at Pressent, write soon, Hoping that you are all well at Home. I remain

Your affectionate Brother

Tom

P.S. I could tell you many Interesting incidents of the Late Battle but I have not the time to write them. Besides if I was to write all I should like to tell you it would fill a good sised Mail Bag.

The rest of the regiment saw heavy combat on the afternoon of July 3 when its remaining companies, along with the First, Second, and Fifth U.S. Cavalries, launched a dismounted attack upon Lee's thinly defended right flank after the repulse of Pickett's Charge. After several hours of fighting, during which the Lancers bore the brunt of the afternoon's battle, Merritt withdrew the Reserve Brigade. Their attack, which petered out when heavy rains started falling late in the afternoon, was bound to fail as it was unsupported by Meade. Capt. Frederick C. Newhall recalled, "A brigade of infantry, backed by an army in position, will stop, if it wishes to, a brigade of cavalry outside of the lines of its own army, devoid of any support, and simply moving against the enemy's flank."[29] The repulse of this attack ended the great Battle of Gettysburg. The two armies fought their way to the banks of the Potomac River in a series of running fights as continuous rains flooded the great river.

The Gettysburg campaign ended on July 13, 1863, with Lee's retreat across the Potomac into Virginia. The Army of the Potomac had a chance to destroy Lee's army, which was pinned on the banks of the flooded river, but Meade's indecision about attacking gave Lee sufficient time to make his escape, although a sharp rearguard action occurred at Falling Waters, Maryland. The Federals pursued the Confederates into Virginia, and the armies eventually made their way back to the banks of the Rappahannock River, from whence they had started the campaign on June 9. There, Smith

Clement Biddle Barclay, the political patron of the Lancers. *Photo courtesy of Brian C. Pohanka, Alexandria, Virginia.*

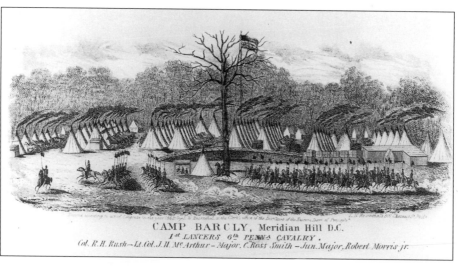

CAMP BARCLY, Meridian Hill D.C.
1st LANCERS 6th PENNA CAVALRY.
Col. R. H. Rush – Lt.Col. J. H. McArthur – Major, C.Ross Smith – Jun.Major, Robert Morris jr.

A lithographic portrayal of Camp Barclay, located on Meridian Hill in Washington, D.C. Note the mounted troopers drilling with their lances. *Photo courtesy of the Library of Congress.*

This photo of Company I, 6th Pennsylvania Cavalry, taken in May 1863, was specifically mentioned by Thomas W. Smith in a letter home. Although there are no known surviving photos of Smith, the author believes that the sergeant standing fifth from the left, with a saber at his side, is Smith. *Photo courtesy of USAMHI.*

Brig. Gen. John Buford, first commander of the Reserve Brigade. Buford referred to the Lancers as his "Seventh Regulars." *Photo courtesy of the National Archives.*

Brig. Gen. Wesley Merritt, second commander of the Reserve Brigade and, later, commander of the First Division of the Cavalry Corps. *Photo courtesy of the National Archives.*

Brig. Gen. Alfred Gibbs, who assumed command of the Reserve Brigade when Merritt was promoted to divisional command. *Photo courtesy of the National Archives.*

Col. Richard H. Rush, first commanding officer of the 6th
Pennsylvania Cavalry. Note Rush's distinctive "dress hat." Smith
mentions this hat in one of his letters home.
Photo courtesy of USAMHI.

Colonel Rush. *Photo courtesy of USAMHI.*

Lt. Col. C. Ross Smith, who served most of his time as a staff officer at Cavalry Corps headquarters. *Photo courtesy of USAMHI.*

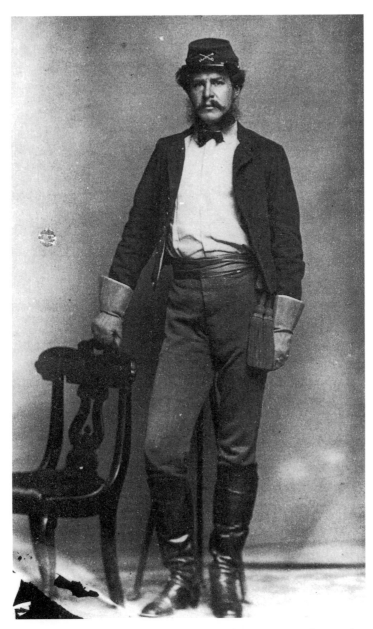

Maj. Robert Morris, Jr., second commanding officer, was captured at Brandy Station on June 9, 1863. Smith named one of his sons for Major Morris.
Photo courtesy of USAMHI.

Maj. George Clymer resigned his commission in the spring of 1863
Photo courtesy of USAMHI.

Maj. John H. Gardiner, the 6th Pennsylvania's third major.
Photo courtesy of USAMHI.

Maj. Henry C. Whelan assumed command of the regiment after Morris fell at Brandy Station. *Photo courtesy of USAMHI.*

Maj. James H. Hazeltine commanded the regiment at the Second Battle of Brandy Station on August 1, 1863. Note the crossed-lance insignia on his kepi. *Photo courtesy of USAMHI.*

Maj. Benoni Lockwood assumed command after Hazeltine was relieved of duty.
Photo courtesy of USAMHI.

Maj. James H. Starr was the commanding officer of Company I for most of the term of Smith's service. *Photo courtesy of USAMHI.*

Capt. William P. C. Treichel, commander of Company A. *Photo courtesy of USAMHI.*

Lt. Albert Payson Morrow, the regiment's last commanding officer, eventually achieved the rank of lieutenant colonel. *Photo courtesy of USAMHI.*

Lt. George Meade, son of the commanding officer of the Army of the Potomac, was commissioned as an officer in Company A. *Photo courtesy of USAMHI.*

Capt. Charles Cadwalader of Company D. *Photo courtesy of USAMHI.*

Capt. Emlen N. Carpenter later commanded Company E. *Photo courtesy of USAMHI.*

Capt. Robert Milligan of Company D. *Photo courtesy of USAMHI.*

Capt. Robert W. Mitchell of Company E. Note the crossed lances on Mitchell's kepi. *Photo courtesy of USAMHI.*

Lt. Theodore Sage, regimental quartermaster, was killed by Mosby's guerrillas during the spring of 1864. *Photo courtesy of USAMHI.*

Chaplain Samuel L. Gracey was the regimental historian of the Lancers.
Photo courtesy of USAMHI.

Smith would have worn the same sort of uniform worn by this unidentified
enlisted man of Company E. *Photo courtesy of USAMHI.*

Pvt. Charles H. Masland of Company E wears one of the unusual hats originially worn by members of the regiment. *Photo courtesy of USAMHI.*

The uniform worn here by Cpl. John Hendrick of Company H is similar to what Smith would have worn in 1862. *Photo courtesy of USAMHI.*

The handsome monument to the Lancers on the South Cavalry Field portions of the Gettysburg National Military Park. *Photo by author.*

The smaller monument of Companies E and I of the Lancers stands outside of Gen. George G. Meade's headquarters on the Gettysburg battlefield. *Photo by author.*

found a few days' respite and time to write home once again. His letter of July 28 reflects the nature of the wild gossip that tended to fly around the headquarters of the Army of the Potomac.

> Head Quarters Armey of the Potomac Warrenton Va
> July 28th 1863

Dear Brother

I received your Letter of the 24th inst yesterday, with the Money enclosed from Mother. I also received at the same time 4 News Papers which you sent me. It was the first mail we had received for 5 or 6 days as the Rebble cavalry had been making a Raid in our rear and cut off all communication between the Armey and Washington.[30]

Last night I overheard a conversation between two Officers high in Command of the Armey of the Potomac. And from their conversation I gathered, that Gen Mead has Received orders from Washington not to attack Lee's Forses nor to cut off their line of Retreat. In fact we are merely to Follow them up, but not molest them in any way untill further Orders. (I mention no names because this is Contraband News).[31]

What in the Devel is the meaning of such Orders, coming at such atime. Surely it can not be that our Government can be so Foolish as to Grant the Rebs an armistice in their pressent Crippled Condition. If so, we might as well throw down our Arms and go Home. I do not know what you will do if you are Drafted. But if you are Drawn, Leave no stone unturned to get exempted.

There is a rumer here today, that there is a Riot going on in Philadelphia to Resist the Draft.[32] I hope that there is no Foundation in it. No more at pressent. Write soon. My love to all.

> Tom

Left Union on the 22nd of July and marched to Upperville Va.[33] Left Upperville on the 23rd of July and marched to Markhams Station on the Manasses Gap Rail Road. Left Markhams Station on the 24th of July and went up in Manasses Gap Expecting a Fight but after some skirmishing the Rebs fell back.[34] We returned to the Station and marched to Salam[35] the same Day. Left Salam on the 25th of July and Marched to the Town of Warrenton, which is about 9 miles from Warrenton Junction.

The armies were stalemated on the banks of the Rappahannock as August began. A series of sharp cavalry engagements developed as the Federal cavalry probed the Confederate defenses to ascertain Robert E. Lee's intentions. On August 1, the second Battle of Brandy Station was fought, again featuring the division of John Buford and the service of the 6th Pennsylvania Cavalry. That day, the Lancers were commanded by Maj. Henry Hazeltine, who did poorly. Buford again led a pincers attack, joined by Kilpatrick's Third Division, and another day-long fight raged over the hills and fields near Brandy Station, including the familiar battlefield of June 9. Smith described the role played by the Lancers in some detail in a letter to his brother Joe.

Head Quarters Armey of the Potomac at
Germantown near Warrenton Junction Va
August 5th/63

Dear Brother

I have just seen a List of the Draft for the 9th [illegible] and I am verry glad to see that your name in not on it. I hope that you may always get as lucky as you did this time. I see that Dick Schofield Franklin Park, John Buck and a great maney other names that I know are among those that are drawn. There is one name on the list Harrison Case. Is that our friend Harry. If so ask him what he is going to do — Fight Pay or Emigrate (how are you Conscript?)

I received your Letter of the 2nd Inst yesterday. I am glad to hear that you are all well at Home.

You made a mistake about that Money that you sent me. I wrote for Two Dollars and you sent me Four.

Our Regiment got pretty Badly Cut up in that Fight at Culpepper the other Day. Major Hazeltine was in command of the Regt,[36] he was ordered by the General in command to charge on a Rebble Battery.[37] As they were advancing to the Charge under a heavy Fire, Hazeltine gave a wrong command and got the men all Bungled up, the Consequense was a Panick. The General [Buford] seeing the Confusion rode out to Ralley them calling out, 6th Pennsylvania what is all this confusion, you are a Regiment I always depended uppon, I never expected to see you Run. Some of the men hallowed out, General tis not our Fault, tis not our fault and Lieut

Whiteford[38] Siezing the Collours, called General the Sixth Pennsylvania never Runs when they have Proper Officers to lead them.

The General answered, No men I know it tis not your Fault, but (turning to Hazeltine) Its your fault you cowardly Son of a Bitch you consider yourself under Arrest Sir. The men gave Three Chears for Lieut Whiteford, and Rallied in time to repulse a Charge of Rebble Cavalry. Hazeltine was sent in to Mead's Head Quarters under Arrest. The Regt lost over 60 men in the Engagement.

We left Warranton Town on the First Inst and marched to this Place. We are now Encamped about two miles from Warrenton Junction at a place called Germantown, we expect to stay here for some time.

This is the meanest Camp that I have been in sinse I left the Peninsula. We cant get a drop of Water fit to drink. The weather is verry warm, very near as bad as Harrisons Landing last summer.

No more at pressent. Give my love to all the Family.

Your affectionate brother
Tom

P.S. We expect the Paymaster here soon. How much money Had from Home
  Susan $5.00
  Mother $44.00
Let me know if that is right.

Tom

Capt Lockwood a Sunday school Teacher is now in command of the Regt.[39]

Chaplain Gracey described the August 1 fight: "Terrific charges were made upon the enemy's line when near Culpeper, in which we drove the cavalry in dismay back upon their supports of infantry, coming up in regular and solid line of battle with their long Enfield rifles, were too strong for our cavalry division, and we were withdrawn in perfect order to Brandy Station, our rearguard resisting the advance of the enemy."[40]

After a few days of rest, the Lancers took the field again, and had another significant skirmish with the Confederate cavalry on August 5. The Reserve Brigade drove a brigade of Confederate cavalry several miles before the pursuit was called off. The Federal cavalry then went into camp near Brandy Station for a well-deserved rest. Smith penned a brief letter home on August 10.

> Head Quarters Armey of the Potomac
> Germantown Va
> August 10th/63

Dear Brother

We got Paid off Yesterday (Sunday). Capt Starr is going to send our Money Home from Washington, by Addams Express. I will send you Fifty Dollars ($50.00). Give Mother $44.00 and Susan $5.00. And the other Dollar you can take to pay the Expressage, and if it does not take it all, send me the Ballance in 3 cts Postage Stamps, not currency. If Capt Starr pays the Expressage in advance, I will return the amount to him, and then you can send me a Dollars worth of Stamps.

I hear that the Regular Bregade of Cavalry composed of the 1st 2nd 5th and 6th U.S. and the 6th P.V. Cavalry Regiments have turned in all their Horses, Arms, and Accoutriments, and are ordered Back to Washington to recruit and get a new outfit.[41] The whole Bregade do not number a Regiment. Capt Starr (Damn his Eyes) has again made application to have us Relieved from Head Quarters, and sent back to the Regiment. This makes the Fourth time that he has done so, and I hope that he will succead no better this time than he has done heretofore. No more at pressent. Write soon. Hoping that you are all as well as I am I remain

> Your affectionate brother
> Tom

By August 15, the time that the Lancers were sent back to Washington, the regiment numbered only two hundred men fit for duty. The summer's campaigning had taken a heavy toll. As the regimental historian noted, "We were ordered to this point to recruit, refit, and reorganize, and after our long campaign, of unprecedented marching and fighting, greatly needed the rest thus secured to us." Sgt. Christian Geisel of Company H wrote home to his sister, "Our whole bregade only numbered 763 men for duty, when we were relieved our Regt 163." Sgt. Lewis Miller of Company L observed that the regiment's "efficiency has been very much impaired since the Battle of

[Brandy Station]. . . . the discipline of the regiment is not as good as when Maj. Morris had command of it. Our commanding officers have been changed so often of late and every one have had a different mode of conducting affairs, which has manifested itself in a perfect state of indifference in the men."⁴² Smith plainly enjoyed the soft job of serving as headquarters escort. Since the army's commanding general rarely stayed in unpleasant or uncomfortable quarters, his escorts shared in the good fortune. Smith plainly stated his unhappiness about the thought of returning to service in the field with the rest of the regiment.

Head Quarters Armey of the Potomac
Sept 2ⁿᵈ 1863

Dear Brother

I received your Letter some Days ago. I have been going to Write to you for some time past, but every thing is so quiet here that I do not know what to write about. The Armey of the Potomac—what is left of them—are mostley scattered along the line of the Rapahanock watching the Rebbles, but between you and I think that more than one half of the old armey have been shipped off to New York and Charleston.⁴³ To be sure we have received and are receiving a great maney Conscripts, but I think that if Lees Armey should advance on us we should have to fall back on to the Defences of Washington without giving them Battle.

I see by the News Papers that the People at Home have an Idea that those Troops at New York are intended for some expedition against the Rebbles.⁴⁴ But it seems to be the general impression here in the Armey that if we succeed in taking Charleston, that those troops in New York are intended by the Government, for an expedition to be sent out to Mexico.⁴⁵

I am glad to hear that Bob has left the City, for I have felt verry uneasy about Him. There are squads of Deserters arriving here at Head Quarters from the North every Day.

How about those Friends of ours that Drew a Prize in the Draft? When you write again let me know what became of them.

For the past two weeks the Weather has been verry Plessant in Day time, but at Night it has been so cold that I wrap myself up in my over coat and blanket and then cant sleep for the cold. Bad Weather for the Ague but so far I have been Luckey enough to keep clear of it, although there are three or four others that have it in our Companey. These Warm Days and Cold nights are a great deal worse than Winter Weather.

Give my love to all the Family. Write soon.

Your brother
Tom

P.S. Ask Mother to send me Five—5—Dollars in your next Letter.

Tom

Things remained relatively quiet throughout the balance of September. Most of the 6th Pennsylvania spent the month refitting in Washington, D.C., while Companies E and I remained on headquarters duty. Finally, Captain Starr got his wish, and Company I was ordered to return to the regiment, which had taken the field again near the old Bull Run battlefield. On October 17, Smith and his comrades from Companies E and I marched to the area around Warrenton and rejoined the regiment.[46] The Lancers went on a reconnaissance that day and on the eighteenth skirmished with the Confederates near Bristoe Station on the Orange and Alexandria Railroad. This mission was part of a general advance by the Army of the Potomac that is known as the Bristoe Station campaign.

The Lancers remained in the field until October 23, when they went into camp at Manassas Junction for a few days. They remained there until the twenty-seventh, when they moved to Germantown, Virginia, taking up position in an "uncomfortable camp."[47] On October 31 the regiment moved to Elk Run, Virginia, where it bivouacked for several days. On November 1, Smith found time to scribble a letter home.

Camp of the 6th Penna Cavalry
at Elkton Va
Nov 1st/63

Dear Brother

I received your letter of Oct 26th. The Plaster was all right. I also received the Press, enclosing Writing Paper some time ago. Mother's Letter, I have not received yet. But I Received a notice from the Post Master at Washington telling me that it was in the Post Office, and that he would send it to me in the Regimental Mail at my own risk if I wished it. I signed the Order and sent it to the P.M. telling him to send the letter, and it is time that I had it now. You should never have any letters Registered to me, as it is a great trouble to get them from the Post Office at Washington. Send them at my risk and I will be responsible for them.

Our Regiment is in Gen Merritt's[48] Bregade. Bufords Division. Which is the First Cavalry Division. The Bregade is composed of the 1st 2nd and 5th Regulars the 1st New York Draggoons, and the 6th Penna Cav.[49] Gen Merritt calls us his 7th Regulars[50] and goes by several names. Some call us the 1st Cav Bregade some the Regular Cav Bregade others the Reserve Cav Bregade. The 6th Regulars belong to the Bregade too, but they are now detached doing duty at Gen Plessonton's[51] Head Quarters.

Joe, I lost all my under clothes the other Day. And there is no place to buy New ones out here. So if it is not too much trouble I wish you Folks at Home would send me some by mail. All I want is Two (2) Good Over Shirts. Get them as Long as Possible. You know the kind. You can sow them up in a Pocket Handkerchief and Direct them to me. It is Cheaper to get them by Mail, than to Buy them our here of the sutlers. Because a Shirt that you would pay two and a half or Three Dollars for at Home we have to pay Six or Seven Dollars for to the Sutlers. If you can get me a Pair of good Cotton Gloves, get them lined with Wool if you can, as I want them for Riding. Send them with the shirts. Let me know how much it all costs and I will Pay you the next time I get Paid.

If any of you can lend me Five (5) Dollars send it to me in a Letter, as I am Broke. No more at pressent. My Love to all. Write soon.

Tom

On November 4, Lt. Theodore Sage, the regimental quartermaster, was ambushed and killed by guerrillas from the command of Maj. John S. Mosby near Elk River, Virginia. Most members of the regiment grieved his loss, as Sage was a popular officer with the men.[52] At the end of November, George Meade attempted a winter movement, known as the Mine Run campaign. Lee set a trap along the banks of the Rapidan but Meade's advance, led by Maj. Gen. Gouverneur K. Warren's Fifth Corps, wisely spotted Lee's ambush and refused to fall into it. The result was an aborted campaign, with the armies going into winter camp along the Rappahannock River in almost the same positions they had held during the previous winter.[53] The

Cavalry Corps played a minor role in this campaign, primarily protecting the Federal flanks from Confederate cavalry attacks.

During the remainder of November, Buford's division remained on picket duty along the Rappahannock. The division, including the Reserve Brigade, skirmished with the Confederate cavalry on November 8, suffering fifty casualties in the process. On November 10, the Cavalry Corps established its camps along the northern bank of the Rappahannock. It continued to picket and scout, and participated in the Mine Run attacks on November 30.[54] During this period, the division underwent a major command shakeup. Buford left with typhoid fever on November 21, and Merritt assumed command as its senior brigadier. Command of the Reserve Brigade fell to Col. Alfred Gibbs of the 19th New York Cavalry.

After the Mine Run affair, the Lancers spent several weeks preparing their permanent winter quarters. The regiment continued to perform its share of picket duty in the winter cold. On December 8, Capt. Emlen N. Carpenter of Company E noted that "seven to ten men froze to death in the trenches—fifteen or twenty rebels were also found frozen to death. Poor fellows—that is worse almost than being shot. The wounded must have suffered horrible torture during those cold nights that we had."[55] This unpleasant but necessary task is described in great detail by Tom Smith in a letter to his brother Joe. We get a real feel for the hardships suffered by the men of the Cavalry Corps as they stood their picket posts in the snow and cold weather.

Camp of the 6th Penna Cavalry

Near Culpeper Va

Dec 13th/63

Dear Brother

I received your Letter of the 8th Inst, enclosing Five Dollars, on the Evening of the 10th Inst. I also Received by the same mail, two News Papers, enclosing each, one plug of Tobacco. The Tobacco is verry good, in fact much better than what we mostly get of the Sutlers. Last evening I received annother Paper with Tobacco.

Joe we have it Damn hard out here, just now. There being only 4 Regiments in our Bregade, for Picket Duty (The 2nd Regulars being on Provost Duty in Culpeper) which brings us on Picket every 4th Day. And as we are generally absent from camp from 32 to 34 hours, we have 2 Days and 3 nights in camp, and 2 days and 1 night on Picket. And I tell you what, setting still on ones Horse from 2 to 4 Hours, these sneaking cold, Frosty nights, ones Blood, Damn near freeses up in his vains. An Infantry man, on Picket, can walk his Post, and by that means keep his Blood in Circulation. But we cannot do so. I wish to God that Mead would hurry up, and eather make a forward moovement, or else fall back to the Line of the Rapahanock, and go into Winter Quarters. It certainly cannot be possible that Mead intends to hold his pressent position. For, Detached as we are, from the main Boddy of the Army, we are liable to be verry much Harressed by the Enemy all winter. If has got to be a common thing, for our Bugles, to Sound to Arms, every Day or Two. When, we Buckel on our Arms, Saddle up our Horses, from Squaddron, and then stand to Horse for 10 or 15 Hours. Which is all caused by the Rebel Cavalry Scoutting around our Pickets, or mayhaps makeing a dash at them.[56] *Damned Plessant aint it.*

I am sorry to hear, that you have so much Trouble, House hunting. It must be very Fatigueing. But I hope that by the time I Direct my next Letter to you, I shall have the Pleassure, of Directing it to your new House.

No more at pressent, give my Love to all the Family. Hoping that you are all well. I am yours &c.

Tom

The army settled into its winter quarters as December dragged on, and the Lancers took their turn on the picket lines. While on picket, the men were vulnerable to enemy fire; it was dangerous for a man to ride along the banks of the Rapidan and Rappahannock Rivers.[57] On the sixteenth, Tom penned his final letter of 1863, offering his brother Joe advice on selecting a house for his family.

Camp of 6th Penna Cavalry
Near Culpeper Va
Dec 16th/63 5 O'clock p.m.

Dear Brother

I have just received yours of the 14th Inst. (We have just come in from Picket). But as there is a mail going out in Half an Hour, I will answer it right away.

In regard to Renting a House for the pressent, do as you think best. But be careful to secure the money in such a way, so that when Property comes down to reasonable Prices, that you can Purchase a House as soon as you get one to suit you. For I think that you will agree with me, that the best investment that you can make out of the money, is to be sure and have a Roof to cover your Heads. That is as soon as you can Purchase to advantage.

In regard to those Signs, or any other old truck that belongs to me, if you can sell them without any trouble, do so. But if you can not sell them, Burn them or do anything else with them that you can, so that you get them out of the way, for I shall never have use for them, or anything else, in that Line of Business any more.[58]

As you say, Three Hundred Dollars will not go far towards Furnishing a House. But you must not be too stylish in your Ideas, rather get, good substancial, and servisable Furniture for the whole House, than to have one Room furnished fancy, and all the rest of the House, a Bare Barn.

No more at pressent. Write soon. My love to all.

> Your affectionate brother
> Tom

On December 25, the Lancers finally settled into their permanent winter quarters. The men got a scare that day as they received orders to mount up, but it turned out to be a false alarm, and the Lancers passed a "pleasant evening" on Christmas.[59]

Eighteen sixty-three had been an arduous and trying year for the regiment, marked by endless marching and fighting. The year also marked the emergence of the Lancers as a force to be reckoned with, earning the respect of John Buford and Wesley Merritt and the proud title of the Seventh Regulars. Buford died of typhoid fever on December 16, and permanent command of the First Cavalry Division fell to his protégé, Wesley Merritt. Command of the Reserve Brigade passed to Col. Alfred Gibbs of the 19th New York Cavalry.

Eighteen sixty-three was also a year of great change for the 6th Pennsylvania Cavalry: Colonel Rush was relieved of duty; Major Morris was captured at Brandy Station and died a lonely death in Richmond's notorious Libby Prison; Maj. George E. Clymer of Company E resigned his commission during the spring; and Major Whelan fell ill from the hardships of the

Gettysburg campaign and left the regiment. Major Hazeltine was relieved of command, and a captain commanded the regiment at year's end. The hated lances had been traded for Sharps carbines, and the men had learned to fight and scout with the best of the Federal cavalry. The Lancers went into their permanent winter quarters with an enviable record and with an optimistic eye toward the future.

Tom Smith finally recovered from the malaria that plagued him the previous winter. In his role as a headquarters escort for the commanding general of the Army of the Potomac, Smith witnessed the great battles at Chancellorsville and Gettysburg from a unique perspective. He saw extensive combat during the fall campaigning and emerged from the year in good health and good spirits, ready for the final year of his enlistment.

CHAPTER SIX

"But Still the Command Was Forward . . ."

1864—Campaigning with Grant

THE ARMY OF THE POTOMAC spent a quiet winter encamped on the old Brandy Station battlefield. In January, the Lancers established their permanent camp near Mitchell's Station on the Orange and Alexandria Railroad, about five miles from the town of Culpeper Court House. Chaplain Gracey recalled, "Very excellent log huts were erected, in regular streets and to uniform dimensions."[1] Some of the men were offered a bounty of one hundred dollars and a furlough to reenlist for the duration of the war. Some reenlisted for the bounty, others for patriotic reasons, as noted by one trooper of Company H: "The reason why I enlisted was I made up my mind to see the thing through to the end for I believe that U. S. Grant will hurry up the cakes in short meter."[2] More than one hundred of the men accepted this offer, but Tom Smith was not one of them.

The 6th Pennsylvania saw some action in early 1864. On February 27, a select force of 550 men, made up of 110 men from each of the five regiments of the Reserve Brigade, participated in a raid on the Virginia Central Railroad near the town of Charlottesville. This long and arduous raid, which commenced at 1:00 A.M. on February 29, was described by Smith in great detail in a letter to his brother Joe. In this raid, the makeshift command had several violent skirmishes and was nearly destroyed by a Confederate ambush, only to be saved from destruction by quick thinking and action by its commanding officer, Brig. Gen. George A. Custer.[3]

> Camp of the 6th Penna Cavalry
> Near Mitchell's Station, VA
> March 3rd 1864

Dear Brother

I received your Letter of Feby 23rd in due time. I also received a Letter of Susan's some time ago. Tell her she must excuse me for not answering her

Letter sooner because I did not feel like writing, and had nothing to write about. Let this answer both of your Letters.

I hope that you will soon be able to get a better sittuation than you have at pressent, but you had Best hold on to your pressent place untill you are sure of a better one.

On the 26th of Febuary we heard that our Infantry were on the moove, and we got orders to be ready to moove at a moments notice. On the evening of the 27th of Feb (at 6 O'clock p.m.) there was a detail of 12 men, from each Company, from each Regt of our Bregade, Ordered to Saddle up with 3 Days Forrage and Rations. Major Trickle took command of the whole,[4] and marched us to Pony Mountain, where we Bivauocked for the night. On the 28th we left Pony Mountain at 11 O'clock a.m. and marched to within one mile of Madison Court House, which we reached at 7 O'clock p.m. We halted here, Fed & cleaned our Horses, got our suppers, and Rested untill midnight (we were joined here by a detail, of the same number of men as our own, from General Custers Bregade,[5] of Kilpatricks Division, we were now told that we were going on a Raid to Charlottsville to try and destroy a large lot of Rebel supplies which the Rebs had stored at this place). Custer now took command of the whole affair. At midnight we saddled up and mooved forward, our Regt on the advance, with orders to Halt for nothing, but if we met pickets and they fired into us, to Charge on them, and drive them before us. We marched forward at a fast gait untill 4 O'clock p.m. on the morning of the 29th, when we had got within about 3 miles of the ford where we intended to cross the Rapidan. Here we met the Rebs Pickets, they Fired into us, we charged them so hard that they did not get annother chance to fire on us untill we got to the ford where we had a pretty sharp skirmish with them. But we drove them and captured two, 6 Horse Waggons loaded with Flour, we now took the Road to Green[e] County Court House driving the Rebs pickets where ever we met them which was quite frequently untill after daylight when they left us aloone.

At 8 O'clock a.m. we reached Green Court House,[6] charged the Town with a yell that served as a morning Revellee for a small Boddy of Rebble Cavalry that were quartered there. They skedaddled in every direction some on Horse Back, but the Largest number of them taking to the Woods on foot. At this Place we captured a Rebel mail, and Destroyed a large number of Saddles, Saddle Trees, Horses, &c.

We now mooved forward at a rappid rate for the next Three or Four Hours without anything of interest occurring. Then we commensed to

meet the Rebel Pickets again. They would fire on us and fall Back, and we
would drive on after them, without returning their shots. We kept on at this
for 3 miles further, when, our Horses being completely fagged out we were
releived by the first Regulars,[7] who took the advance, and we fell in the rear
of Bregade.

Two miles further and we came to the Ravenna River,[8] there was a
Cavalry camp on this side of the River, but we never Halted. We charged
right through their camp, and they fled to the Woods in every direction
leaveing their Horses, Arms, and Acccoutrements of every description
scattered promiscuously around camp, which prooved that they were taken
completely by supprise and that they never drempt that there were any
Yanks within 60 Miles of them.

It was now 2 O'clock p.m. We had been in the saddle 14 Hours, and had
Rode over 60 Miles without Halting. But still the Command was Forward.
After Watering our Horses in the Ravenna, we crossed the Bridge, and
pushed on for about 2 miles further when they commensed shelling us
from some 8 or 10 peices of Artillery, this checked our advance, and even
compelled us to fall back a little out of Range. We now discovered that they
were receiving Reenforsements of Infantry, by Rail, (supposed to have
come eather from Orange Court House, or Gordonsville). It was now
decided by our Officers, to divide our small forse into two collumms and
do them as much dammage as possible, before we were compelled to fall
back for good. Capt Ash[9] of the 5th Regulars took a By Road to the Left
through a Woods, with about two Hundred men, and the Rest of us
mooved forward on the Road that we were on. We had not gone more than
a quarter of a mile, when we heard a devil of an explosion on our Left. Our
collumn Halted and Gen Custer went up on a small Hill to Reconnoiter, he
discovered Capt Ash's command on the Back Track, and also discovered
the Rebel infantry marching in three collumns on our Left to get posession
of the Bridge in our Rear, and thus cut off our retreat. So we weeled about
and made for the Bridge as fast as our tired out Horses could carry us. We
now recrossed the Bridge and then set fire to it. We also Burnt a Large mill,
full of Flour and Grain at this point. (When Capt Ash took the Road to the
Left, the first that he knew, he was right into a Rebbel Artillery Camp. He
blew up 7 caisons, when he found that the Reb Infantry were closing in on
him. He then Rallied his men and cut his way out, In this Fight he Lost one
man Killed, and 4 men wounded, all of the 5th Cavalry. The whole affair did
not Last scarsely 5 minuts).

It was now 5 O'clock p.m. and the weather was verry Disagreable, and it was commensing to Rain. So we took the Back track, our Regiment acting as rear Guard. Some Rebel Cavalry followed us up, but when ever they would come too close, we would weel about and charge them, when they would always show us their Heals. At 8 O'clock p.m. it was Raining verry Hard, and Dark as the Devil. About this time we lost our Road in a thick and tangled Woods and after wandering about for about two Hours we found it would be impossible for us to get our Artillery through so we come to the conclusion to dismount and stand to Horse where we were untill Day Light, it continued to Rain verry hard all night.

The next morning at Day Light (March 1st) having found the Right Road, we mounted and mooved on again. We were now Fired upon by small Bodies of Rebel Cavalry (as we advanced) from every cover. We had made about 3 miles, and were passing through a thick Woods when our Company being the extreme Rear Guard, we were attacked by a Boddy of Rebel Cavalry.[10] We succeeded in Holding them in check untill the ballance of our Regiment came back to our assistance, when we charged them and drove them off.

In this Skirmish Sergt Wright[11] (My Butty) received a severe Pistol shot Wound in the Hip. When we came to Green Court House we destroyed a Large quantity of Wheat, and Burnt annother Flour mill. We then went on untill we came to a cross Roads, going to two different Fords on the Rapidan. The one on the left going to Banks Ford where we crossed before, was held by a Boddy of Rebel Cavalry. So we took the Road to the right which went to Berthels Ford.[12] We had marched about 5 miles on this Road, and had got pretty near to the Ford, when we discovered that it was held by Cavalry, Artillery, and Infantry. General Custer said that we could cut our way through at Banks Ford, easier than we could at this, so we wheeled about again, and started for Banks Ford which we crossed without opposition (the Rebel Cavalry having taken the River Road to Bertels Ford when they Discovered that we had gone to that Place). We Burnt another Large Mill at this place, and then mooved on to Madison Court House which we Reached at dark. We then went about 3 miles further crossing the Robison River,[13] where we watered our jaded Horses.

We then halted for two hours, to Feed our Horses and get something to eat for ourselves. At 10^{1}/$_{2}$ O'Clock we mounted again, and marched to Camp which we reached at 3 O'clock a.m. on the morning of the 2nd, soaked with Rain, Covered with mud, and completely tired out.

We brought in with us, some 30 prissoners, about 50 Contrabands,[14] and between Three and Four Hundred Fine Horses. Besides this every man had his Saddle Loaded with chickens, Turkeys, Ducks, Geese, Hams, &c.

We could have taken Hundreds of Prissoners if we had been so minded. But that was not our object, we did not want to be encumbered with them. So we took no more than what actually fell into our hands. I hear that Kilpatrick started on a Raid on the Left the same Day that we started on the Right.[15]

No more at pressent. I am right well. Give my Love to all the Familey. Write soon.

Your brother

Tom

P.S. You must not expect annother letter from me for the next Six Months after writing all this. I Received Father's Letter today. Let this answer all.

Tom

Of the feint that got the entire column safely across the river, General Custer reported, "The enemy discovered the change in my movements, but too late to profit thereby. A force of 500 cavalry, which had been hurried up from Burton's Ford to intercept us, only arrived in time to see my rearguard safely across the river." One Lancer noted that Companies I and M "skirmished with the enemy all day."[16] Smith was engaged in this fighting all day long. Custer crowed:

My command returned to its camp without having suffered the loss of a man. While on this expedition it marched upwards of 150 miles, destroyed the bridge over the Rivanna River, burned 3 large flouring mills filled with grain and flour, captured 6 caissons and 2 forges, with harnessses complete; captured 1 standard bearing the arms of Virginia, over 50 prisoners, and about 500 horses, besides bringing away over 100 contrabands. A large camp of the enemy was also captured and destroyed near Charlottesville. The conduct of the officers and men of my command was all that I could desire.[17]

Capt. Theodore S. Garnett, one of Stuart's aides-de-camp, gave an account of the fight.

after traveling less than a mile from our "ambush," [we] met a squadron of Custer's brigade coming toward them. Gen. Stuart at once ordered a "Charge," and in another moment the Yankees were retreating at full speed, and orders were sent to the 2nd [Virginia Cavalry] Regiment . . . to come up at a gallop.

In less than five minutes, Co. K [of the 1st Virginia Cavalry] was seen hurrying back closely followed by a charging squadron of Yankees, which was only induced to draw rein at sight of our advancing column. But now the range of hills in our front was literally swarming with Yankee cavalry, which deployed right and left on either side of the road, and pushed forward a heavy line of skirmishers. . . . The Yankees were now getting ready to dash upon us, and in another moment they commenced a charge . . . [they] came within easy pistol shot of Gen. Stuart . . . , to whom they gave chase. The General seeing that they could not get at him over the fence, cantered along down the lane rather too leisurely, turning every now and then to his ordnance officer and saying, "Shoot that fellow, Grattan! Shoot him!" pointing to a Yankee who was plugging away at both of them.[18]

Maj. Gen. Alfred Pleasonton, commanding the Cavalry Corps, informed Custer of "his entire satisfaction at the result of your expedition, and the gratitude he has felt at the prompt manner in which the duties assigned you have been performed."[19] Custer's raid was a diversion for a planned raid by Brig. Gen. Judson Kilpatrick and Col. Ulric Dahlgren, intended to free the Union prisoners held in Libby Prison. However, while the Kilpatrick/Dahlgren Raid failed and led to the death of its gallant leader, Dahlgren, Custer's raid was a success.

After the conclusion of the raid, the 6th Pennsylvania returned to its camp, where it spent a quiet March picketing a front of about eight miles and guarding a signal station atop Cedar Mountain.[20] In the meantime, the Army of the Potomac was reorganized into fewer, larger infantry corps, and the Federal forces received a new commanding officer, Lt. Gen. Ulysses S. Grant, formerly commander of all of the Federal forces in the western theater. The grim and unbending westerner was a fierce warrior, bent on winning the war at all costs. Brig. Gen. Rufus Ingalls, the chief quartermaster of the Army of the Potomac, met Grant and keenly observed to General Meade, "I tell you, Meade, Grant means business."[21]

Grant planned for coordinated simultaneous movements by the major Federal armies, designed to prevent the Confederacy from shifting forces to meet threats. The plan included a spring campaign for the Army of the Potomac in the east, a combined move on Atlanta by the Armies of the Tennessee, Cumberland, and Ohio, and an advance up the Shenandoah Valley by a force commanded by Maj. Gen. David Hunter. Among the many changes made by Grant was the replacement of Alfred Pleasonton as commander of the Cavalry Corps. Grant evidently hated Pleasonton, for his removal was without ceremony and with no little insult.[22] In April Grant replaced him with Maj. Gen. Philip Sheridan, his friend and protégé who had little experience with the mounted arm. The First Division also got a new commander, Brig. Gen. Alfred T. A. Torbert, another former infantry officer. One of Merritt's Regulars astutely observed that Torbert was "a handsome dashing fellow, at this time, a beautiful horseman, and as brave as a lion; but his abilities were hardly equal to such large commands."[23]

Smith's prediction that he would not write home again for six months quickly proved wrong, as the following letter to his sister Jane demonstrates. In this letter, Smith reports on the fate of the regiment's highest-ranking officers, illustrating the high level of attrition among them.

> Camp of the 6th Penna Cavalry
> Near Mitchells Station Va
> April 5th 1864

Dear Sister Jennie

I received Joes Letter of the 17th ult, and yours of the 21st all in due time. I am verry glad indeed, that you and Susan and Joe, have got settled down at last, and that you are all together. I hope that you will be well suited in your new Boarding House. When you write again, you must let me know all about the Familey that you are Boarding with, how many there is in the Familey, what kind of People they are, if there are any other Boarders besides yourselves &c.

Tell Joe that Sam Wright is getting along verry well, he is in one of the Hospitals at Washington. It was only a flesh wound (a Pistol Ball) in the Thigh that he received, but I guess he can manage to make it keep him out of danger for the Ballance of his term of Servise.[24]

We are in the 1st Cavalry Division commanded by Brigadear General Merritt and 3rd Bregade commanded by Colonel Gibbs of the 1st New York Draggoons.[25] Our Regiment is commanded by Major Treichel. The following is a list of the Field Officers of our Regiment, and what has become of them sinse the Regiment has been organised. Colonel Rush Transfered to Invalid Corps.

Lieutent Colonel McArther ordered to his own Regiment (the 2nd U.S. Cavalry)[26] now on detached duty in the Army of the Cumberland. Major Smith[27] now Colonel of the Regiment. But on detached duty acting Adjutant General at Cavalry Corps Head Quarters.

Major Morris. Taken prissoner at the Fight at Beverly Ford[28] and died in Libby Prisson at Richmond.

Major Gardiner.[29] Resigned.

Major Hazeltine. Resigned.[30]

Major Whelen. Died at his home in Philadelphia about 2 months ago.[31]

Major Lockwood Resigned.[32]

Major Clymer. Resigned.[33]

Major Treichel pressent commanding Regiment.

Major Starr. Home on Furlough.[34]

The veterans of our Regiment (about 170 one Hundred and Seventy in number) are Home on Furlough. But their time will be up, and we expect them back in 6 or 8 Days.

As the Army of the Potomac is being consolidated into three Corps, I think it is verry likely that the Cavalry Corps will be broken up, and one division of Cavalry attached to each Corps. If so I guess our Division will be attached to the 5th Corps, Commanded by Major General Warren.[35]

We are having some verry Rough Weather just now. It has Rained nearly every Day sinse that Big Snow Storm we had some two or three weeks ago.

I must now close, give my Love to all. Write soon again. Your last Letter was verry chearful and Interesting. I hope that you all are in good helth. For my part, I am well, Hearty, and in good Spirrits notwithstanding the Bad Weather.

Your affectionate brother

Tom

Sheridan received his orders to prepare to move on April 22, and his troopers were issued 150 rounds each as well as subsistence rations. As Sgt. Christian Geisel of Company H wrote just before the march began, "All the way from our camp back to Brandy Station the country is covered with camps as far as the eye can reach, and the troops all in fine condition and good spirits." John T. Baynes, another member of Company H, noted, "We will go down and give 'Old Lee' a hell of a thrashing for we are just the boys to do it."[36]

Ten days later the Cavalry Corps began scouting the major fords over the Rapidan River. At midnight on May 3–4, it began crossing the river as the Army of the Potomac moved into the Wilderness.[37] Grant's campaign took the army over where it had suffered a disastrous defeat exactly a year earlier under Hooker. As the move neared, Smith found time to write a letter home wherein he accurately analyzed the role of the cavalry in the coming Wilderness campaign. The same day, Geisel wrote home to his sister Louisa, "Gen. Grant is in no hurry about moving, but I think when he starts once there will be some warm work to be done. . . ." Geisel did not realize how right he was.[38]

Camp of the 6th Penna Cavalry
Near Culpeper Va May 3rd/64

Dear Sister

I received your Letter yesterday, and am verry glad to hear that you are enjoying good Helth. I also received a Letter from Joe some time ago.

We mooved out of our Winter Quarters about two weeks ago, and mooved back to within a mile of Culpeper where we are now encamped. We are under marching orders, and are expecting the Army to moove every Hour.[39] For the last two weeks we have drawn nothing but the marching Ration, which consists of Coffee, Sugar, Pork and Hard Tack.

I do not think that there will be much cavalry Fighting in the coming campaign. As our cavalry was never in such poor condition as it is at Pressent. Our Horses are the most miserable looking Kanks, that you ever laid eyes on, and only Half of the men mounted at that. Our Regiment has only two Hundred and twenty five men mounted. The Rebel Cavalry, are reported to be in splendid condition, they having been Laying back and recruiting their Horses, While we have been on out Post duty, Raiding and Reconnoitering, all Winter.

Our Division is now commanded by General Tolbert.[40] Our Bregade by General Merritt, and our Regiment by Major Starr.

General Grant is having Culpeper Fortified by Earth Works and Entrenchments thrown upon every Knoll and Ridge of Rising Ground.

I must now close as it is getting late (10 O'clock p.m.) and we are under orders to be ready to moove at day Break. But I guess the order will be countermanded as it is Raining Hard just now.[41]

Tell Jane to write to me and let me know how she likes her new occupation. What her duties are, and how she likes them &c.[42]

You and Joe must write often and let me know how you are getting along. No more at pressent.

Your affectionate brother
Tom

P.S. I have Wrote three Letters, one to Father, one to Mother and one to Ben. All directed to No. 411 Lombard St. and I have Received no Answer to any of them.

On the morning of May 4, John P. Kepner of Company I noted in his diary, "The inspiring music of our Hd Qrs Band rang loud and clear on the morning air at 2 a.m. calling the warriors from sweet repose to pack up for the campaign just opening."[43] The Army of the Potomac plunged into the Virginia countryside. The Battle of the Wilderness raged for two days, with both armies suffering huge casualties in a blind, close fight. The Lancers played no role in the main battle; they spent May 6 supporting an attack by Custer's brigade of the First Cavalry Division.

As the fighting in the Wilderness wound down, Grant decided to move the Army of the Potomac around Lee's flank by way of the important crossroads town of Spotsylvania Court House. The Cavalry Corps was given the task of clearing the roads. A ramshackle hotel called Todd's Tavern stood at the strategic intersection of the Brock and Catharpin Roads. The Federal horsemen led the advance but ran into heavy resistance from Confederate cavalry. If the Federal troopers could push through, they could win the race for Spotsylvania Court House and force Lee to attack the Army of the Potomac.[44]

Initially, the men of the Reserve Brigade were to guard the Cavalry Corps wagon trains, but when the fighting grew heavy, Merritt sent for them. The Lancers saw a great deal of fighting at Todd's Tavern on May 7. With the Lancers leading the initial attacks, the Reserve Brigade spent the entire day sparring with the Confederate brigades of Wade Hampton and Fitzhugh

Lee near Todd's Tavern. One newspaper reporter recorded that the "air seemed filled with leaden missiles from either side." Lee recorded, "A severe combat raged until dark."[45] Reserve Brigade commander Col. Alfred Gibbs had his horse shot out from under him, and the Lancers took heavy casualties, including the killing of the regimental adjutant and the serious wounding of Major Starr, who was hit in the face by a pistol ball.[46]

Reinforced by infantry of the Fifth Corps, the Federal cavalry finally drove the Confederates from their strong defensive positions near the tavern. The *Philadelphia Inquirer* reported, "General Merritt had the right, where the fire was the hottest. The Reserve Brigade suffered the most, as it was most hardly pressed, and most nobly did they meet the desperate onslaught. Our cavalry were all dismounted, for the contest occurred mostly in thick woods, where horses could not be used to advantage."[47] While Todd's Tavern was a tactical victory for the Federal troopers, the delay it created permitted Lee to move his infantry to Spotsylvania Court House, where it took up an imposing defensive position. Instead of forcing Lee to attack him, Grant would either have to attack Lee, or he would have to find a way to flank Lee out of his strong position. Grant chose to attack.

As this drama played out, the Cavalry Corps spent several days at Todd's Tavern, guarding the roads while Grant moved his infantry onto Spotsylvania Court House, where a great and bloody battle began on May 8. The fighting quickly bogged down into static positions—bloody direct frontal assaults against solidly entrenched positions. The battle would rage for almost ten days before Grant finally broke contact and sidled around Lee's flank toward Richmond. On May 10, while the battle continued and as the regiment was preparing its morning meal, the shrill whine of falling artillery shells permeated the air.

After a brief skirmish, the Cavalry Corps set off on a raid toward Richmond, with the Lancers taking the advance. On May 11, the Federals found the entire Confederate Cavalry Corps massed in front of them. This culminated in the great Battle of Yellow Tavern. After a huge melee in which J. E. B. Stuart was mortally wounded, the Federals brushed the Confederates out of their way and continued toward Richmond, stopping within three miles of the city. Geisel wrote, "What a moment of excitement, in the cold, damp hours of a May morning to see ten thousand strong men halted, and waiting in breathless suspense." Facing the fortifications around Richmond, Sheridan realized that the defenses were too strong to be broken by a cavalry raid, and he turned his column away from the Confederate capital.[48] Another battle with the Confederates occurred on the twelfth while the raid continued down the Peninsula, returning Smith to the malarial swamps he first saw in 1862.

By the end of May, the Army of the Potomac had crossed the North Anna River and was working its way toward the James. On May 31, Merritt had a sharp engagement with the Confederate cavalry near the old Mechanicsville battlefield of the Peninsula campaign. Merritt's attack drove Confederate infantry and cavalry almost a mile before he called off the pursuit.[49] By June 1, the two armies faced each other across an elaborate network of trenches at Cold Harbor and a stalemate developed, with the Confederate infantry launching desperate attacks against Merritt's strong line of dismounted troopers.

On June 2, the Federal cavalry reached Bottom's Bridge over the Chickahominy River, not far from Cold Harbor and the old battlefields of McClellan's 1862 campaign. The Federals threw up entrenchments, heavily picketed the river, and spent the night there, drawn up in line of battle. While there, Smith found time to write home to his sister Jane. This short, hastily written letter reflects the heavy fighting faced by the Federal cavalry during Grant's overland campaign.

In line of battle Near Bottoms Bridge Va
June 3rd 1864

Dear Sister

I Received your Letter of the 23rd ult. You must excuse me for not writing sooner but when I went into the First Days fight at Todds Tavern, I Destroyed all of the Letters that I had about my Person,[50] and by that Means Lost your directions so that when I had a chance to write Home I could not do so on that account. I have only had two chances to Write Home sinse the Campane opened. The mail carrier is on the line now collecting Letters so I have only a few moments to write in.

I was on the Raid,[51] and with the Regiment ever sinse the Campane opened. 21 Days out of 29 we have been in Fight. Our Regiment have lost 97 men, all told, including 7 Officers.

I Received a Letter from Susan, and one from Father some time ago. Let this answer all of them. I am well and as yet unhurt. I have been verry lucky so far and hope to continue so.

Sergt Pennington[52] and Sergt Reinhart[53] have both been wounded. I am the only Sergt left in the Company with the exception of Quartermaster & Commissary Sergt. But they do not go into fight.

You must keep in good Spirrits, and give yourselves no uneasiness about me.

There is no use of borrowing trouble, tis time enough when it comes. I must now close. Write soon and send me your Directions. Give my Love to all the Familey.

> Your affectionate brother
> Tom

P.S. Please send me a Pass Book about the size of pattern, not too thick.

Infantry finally relieved the cavalry on June 4, and the Reserve Brigade joined the rest of the Cavalry Corps on another raid, this time toward a Confederate supply depot near Gordonsville. This raid culminated in the great battle of Trevilian Station, wherein the Confederate and Federal mounted corps spent June 11 and 12 fighting at close quarters. During this fight, George Custer's small brigade walked into a Confederate trap and was nearly destroyed before it cut its way out. The Lancers were heavily engaged the whole day on June 11, suffering at least forty-three casualties. Capt. Frank Furness of Company F was awarded the Medal of Honor at Trevilian for carrying a box of ammunition "across an open space swept by the enemy's fire to the relief of an outpost whose ammunition had become almost exhausted, but which was thus enabled to hold its important position."[54] The gray horsemen fell back, with Sheridan in hot pursuit. On the twelfth, the Reserve Brigade made a mounted charge against Confederate rifle pits, with the Lancers losing another thirty-six men in a fight that "raged furiously." Sheridan finally realized that further attacks were futile and withdrew; according to the Confederates, "The enemy are driven back in confusion until night and the thickness of the country prevents further pursuit. Enemy appears to be retiring in disorder." In his after-action report, Torbert praised the Regulars: "During the engagement the Reserve Brigade fought with more than their usual desperation, driving the enemy before them."[55]

After several days of hard marching, the Federal cavalry marched through the Spotsylvania Court House battlefield, where they saw "The debris of the battle strewed the ground; large trees were seen cut nearly in two; scarred and shattered by solid shot, shell, and musket balls, while heavy lines of earthworks marked where the severest charges were made and resisted. The graves of those who fell on this terrible field were on every hand."[56]

By the nineteenth, the Lancers reached Dunkirk on the Mattapony River. On the twenty-first, the Reserve Brigade went into camp for a brief rest. As Chaplain Gracey noted, "Here some of us are said to have bathed and changed our clothes for the first time in two weeks, the latter part of which seems more credible than the first, for, ever since June 7th, when we started on the Trevillian raid, we had marched daily at 5 o'clock p.m., not reaching camp often not until after dark, after such days of heat and dust as choke one to look back upon. All our wardrobe was on our backs, so that our camp here, where our wagons rejoined us, was an oasis."[57]

After several restful days, the Lancers moved to a new camp near Charles City Court House on June 25. That night, after standing to horse for several hours in the blazing summer sun, the Lancers marched to Wilson's Wharf on the James River, where they stayed until the twenty-eighth. Smith again found time to pen a few lines home to his sister Susan. In his letter, he accurately described the travails of nonstop campaigning and the toll it took on the officers and men of the regiment.

> Camp of 6th Penna Cavalry
> Near Fort Powhattan on James River
> June 27th 1864
>
> Dear Sister
>
> I received your Letter of 11th Inst. Fathers Letter of 13th inst, Martha's Letter of the 4th Inst. Last evening and this morning I Received your Letter of the 21st Inst. Also that package from Jennie which is verry acceptable just at this time, as I was completely out of such articles. This is the first mail that we have received sinse the 4th of this month, we have not got near all of our back mail yet, but we are expecting more of it in, everry moment.
>
> I suppose that you know by the Papers that we have just returned from our second raid. We started from Old Church Tavern on the 7th inst. making a Raid around by Gordonsville Destroying a Large Lot of Rebbel supplies and Destroying and tareing up Rail Roads. But the chief advantage gained was by cooperating with Gen Hunter,[58] by Drawing the

Rebels away from his front, thus giving him a great advantage over the Rebs of which I suppose he took advantage.

On the 11th and 12th we fought the Rebs at Trevilian Station on Virginia Central R.R. from morning to night of both Days. In this engagement our Regiment Lost One (1) Commissioned Officer and Sixty Six (66) Enlisted Men.

On the 20th we reached the White House just in time to meet the Rebel Cavalry and foil their Designes on our waggon trains at that Point on the 25th we succeded in getting our waggon trains all safe through to this point. We have now got them all across the river and the cavalry are comming to cross to join Grant. We have to cross every thing in ferry Boats which is a verry tedious operation. I suppose by the time we get across, we will be considered sufficiently recuperated for annother Desperate expedition of some kind. Sinse the Campain opened our Regiment have lost, in Killed, Wounded and Missing Ten (10) Commissioned Officers and One Hundred and Sixty Six (166) Enlisted Men. I have been in every fight and skirmish that the Regiment has been in, and have had some verry narrow escapes from being taken prissoner and in other ways. But so far I have been lucky enough to escape Scott free. I am in good helth, and in not verry bad spirrits considering the Hot Wether.

It is useless for me to try to give you any of the details of what I have seen and been through sinse this Campain opened. For I might write a book as large as a Familey Bible, and then call it the Preface. I wish you would let the rest of the Familey know that I am well, for I have not got time to write more than one Letter.

I wish you would send me a set of Orderly Sergts Shevrons for the sleeve. Get them as narrow striped as possible. Also 2 and 3/4 yards of Braid for pants. When you send them let me know how much they Cost.

We are expecting to draw Cloathing soon, and I hope it will not be long a comming, for I was never so Ragged in my Life as I at Pressent.

No more at Pressent, give my Love to all the Family. Hoping to hear from you soon, I Remain

Your affectionate brother
Tom

P.S. Why does not Joe write. He has not wrote to me sinse he left City Hall.

Smith requested the new chevrons for good reason. On June 4, he was promoted to first sergeant of Company I for which he received a pay raise.[59]

On the twenty-ninth, the regiment was ferried across the James River and marched east. It finally went into camp on July 3 for a well-deserved rest. Despite the terrible heat, the Lancers enjoyed the nearly month-long respite. During this period, Major Starr, commanding the regiment, requested that the Lancers be sent home to Pennsylvania to recruit. General Meade rejected this request, meaning that the unit "was but a skeleton of a regiment for the rest of the war."[60] Of course, his decision was highly unpopular with the men.

> Camp of the 6th Penna Cavalry
> Near City Point on James River
> July 13th 1864

Dear Sister

I Received Jennies letter of the 5th Inst and that Package of Shevrons that you sent to me last Evening. The Shevrons are just the thing, and could not have been made to please me better. When you Write again let me know how much they cost, and I will Send you the money as soon as I get paid. I cannot pay you now, because I have no money myself. But there is 4 months Pay due us, and as soon as I get that, I shall pay you all that I owe you.

We are still encamped the same place as when I last Wrote to you, Picketing in the Rear, and Flank of the Army. We went out on Picket on the morning of the 9th to Prince George Court House and Returned to Camp last Evening. While on Picket on the night of the 11th we were attacked by Guarrillas and had two men wounded.

Jennie does not mention in her Letter wether she has secured another situation yet, or not. Let me know in your next.

It is rumored here that the Rebs are makeing a big Raid through Maryland. And I suppose that there is some truth in it.[61] But I do not think that they will succeed in making Grant abandon his Works here in front of Petersburg which I take to be their object. I wish that they would send us up to Maryland after the Rebs, for I think that I could live better in Maryland for the ballance of my term of enlistment, than I can down in this Barren and God Forsaken country.

Major Starr has recovered from his Wounds,[62] and has returned to, and is now in command of the Regiment.

No more at pressent. My Love to you and all the Family. Write soon again.

Your affectionate brother

Tom

P.S. I wrote a Letter to Joe a few days ago.

Smith correctly assessed the motivation behind Early's raid into Maryland. Knowing that only a bold stroke could break the Federal stranglehold on his army at Petersburg, Lee ordered the raid in a desperate effort to relieve the relentless pressure on his front, but the gambit failed. Grant, who had been besieging Petersburg since June 18, detached only the Sixth Corps and two divisions of the Cavalry Corps to chase Early, and the balance of the Army of the Potomac remained in its siege lines. If Petersburg fell, so too would Richmond because if Lee's lines of supply were severed, the Confederate capital would have to be evacuated.

Smith got his wish. The Lancers were sent into the Valley to search for Early's army. Unfortunately, Smith's correspondence ceased with his letter of July 13. There is no detailed record of his duty in Sheridan's Valley campaign, but his service records indicate that he was present with the regiment during July, August, and September.[63]

After fighting and picketing around Petersburg during the remainder of July, the Cavalry Corps marched into the Valley at the beginning of August and spent the fall months in hard campaigning. Company I "participated in all the operations of the First Cavalry Division during [July and August 1864] and was engaged in the battles of Deep Bottom, Kearnystown, Newtown and Smithfield."[64]

Smith saw his last combat on August 28, when the Reserve Brigade engaged a strong force of infantry and artillery along the banks of the Opequon Creek. After nearly a full day's fighting, the Confederates were driven off. On September 9, the regiment was sent to rest and refit at a remount camp about two miles from Harpers Ferry at a place called Pleasant Valley. Orders were issued for the soon-to-be discharged members of the regiment to turn in their mounts for the benefit of the dismounted veterans of the

Reserve Brigade. A member of the 6th Pennsylvania observed, "They are discharged singly and in squads, just as their time expires." Badly depleted by the discharges, the Lancers missed the balance of the fall's campaigning. On October 13, 1st Sgt. Thomas W. Smith was mustered out of the 6th Pennsylvania Cavalry when his term of enlistment expired. He was paid seventeen dollars in back wages, receiving the additional one hundred dollars he was owed later, and started on his way home, his war over.[65]

Epilogue

WHILE MERELY A "skeleton of a regiment," the Lancers served with Sheridan's Cavalry Corps for the remainder of the war. They returned to the Reserve Brigade on January 15, 1865, having finally completed their refitting at Pleasant Valley. The regiment's officer corps had been decimated. Col. Charles L. Leiper, the regiment's last commanding officer, wrote to Governor Curtin just before the Lancers took the field again that many of the current batch of officers had "no idea of discipline and of the simplest duties of an officer. . . . We are obliged to keep them, because if they were court-martialed, this regiment would be left with but three-four officers, and that number would be insufficient to work it." Despite these problems, the remaining Lancers took the field as the 1865 campaign season began. After the destruction of Early's Army of the Valley on March 1, the Cavalry Corps returned to the Army of Potomac. Completing a long march across Virginia, the Lancers finally arrived at Grant's siege lines at Petersburg on March 25, joining the Cavalry Corps' march west toward the crucial crossroads of Five Forks.[1]

On March 31, the regiment participated in the important battle of Dinwiddie Court House, wherein Sheridan's men almost suffered an embarrassing defeat. As the regimental historian noted, "the enemy . . . were now seeking to break up our force and drive us away from Dinwiddie, and send us reeling back upon the Army of the Potomac. They were making good headway, they thought, in this intent, when we were ordered to the rescue." Leading a fierce counterattack, they made a dismounted charge against the cream of Lee's best infantry, breaking the Confederate battle lines. However, the 6th Pennsylvania, depleted to only six companies before the battle, sustained still more casualties in the heavy fighting, including Lt. Col. Albert P. Morrow, who was severely wounded in the thigh.[2]

On April 1, the critical Battle of Five Forks was fought. The Union infantry launched its attack supported by dismounted Federal cavalrymen. The depleted Lancers led the Union advance to Five Forks, where its men dismounted and spearheaded Sheridan's attack on the Confederate breastworks. Only forty-eight officers and enlisted men remained in the regiment as it went into battle that morning.[3] The Federal attack shattered the Confederate lines and cleared the way for Grant's breakout from Petersburg, finally causing the fall of Richmond after four long years of war. Five Forks was the final fight for this superb regiment. The next day, Wesley Merritt, recognizing that their ranks were too thin to permit them to handle anything more than headquarters duty, pulled the surviving Lancers from the line and made them his headquarters guard.

Thus ended the fighting career of one of the first and best of the Federal cavalry regiments raised in the Civil War. Rush's Lancers had come a long way, from inexperienced socialites to the hard-fighting "Seventh Regulars," a name the men of the 6th Pennsylvania wore proudly. A handful of Lancers participated in the Grand Review of the Army of the Potomac after the war and were mustered out of service later in 1865, leaving a fighting record as memorable as that of any Union cavalry regiment. Sheridan himself noted in 1866, "No organization in either the regular or volunteer service enjoyed a more enviable reputation in every respect."[4]

Throughout the course of the war, 172 members of the 6th Pennsylvania died of either wounds or disease. Owing largely to their extended tour of duty as the Army of the Potomac's headquarters detail, only eight of those men came from the ranks of Company I.[5] Nevertheless, the war took its toll on the Lancers. Of the men who led the regiment in the early days of the war, only two of the original field officers remained in command of elements of the regiment at war's end. Officers died, suffered the effects of hard service in the field, or were wounded in battle.

In 1888, a handsome monument to the Lancers was unveiled on the South Cavalry Field portion of the battlefield at Gettysburg, commemorating the role played by the 6th Pennsylvania in the long and severe fight on the afternoon of July 3, 1863. The monument depicts the distinctive lances in full scale, including the small scarlet pennants that tipped them. A second, smaller monument to the men of Companies E and I was erected just behind Meade's headquarters and was dedicated the same day. Many members of the regiment, both enlisted men and officers, made the trek to Gettysburg for the dedication of the monument and to hear the dedication speech by Capt. Frederick C. Newhall, delivered on October 14. Unfortunately, Thomas W. Smith was not among the veterans who made the trek to Gettysburg that day.

Upon his discharge from the army, the twenty-six-year-old Smith returned home to Philadelphia, where he resumed his career as an upholsterer. He rented a room in a boarding house owned by Charles F. Sweet,

who observed that upon his discharge from the army, Smith's health
was poor: "I distinctly remember that he was much broken down in health
and was crippled with Rheumatism, which I ascertained from conversa-
tions with him was contracted while in the U.S. service from exposure. At
that time he was in my opinion totally unable to do any hard manual labor
and for a year or more he was at very frequent intervals laid up and unable
to go out of the house."[6] Sweet noted that this disability later forced Smith
to give up the upholstery business. When Smith applied for a military pension in the late 1880s, he wrote, "When I came out of the army I went to
work at James Henry Armes Carpet Store on Chestnut Street . . . for a short
time at upholstering but the Rheumatism got so bad that I had to give it
up and did not do anything untill August 1867." In 1867, Smith started his
own upholstering business and worked at it until the time of his pension
application, hiring workers to perform those tasks his rheumatism pre-
vented him from doing.[7]

Smith boarded with Sweet for nearly seven years and then spent several
years residing in various locations throughout Philadelphia. On November 9, 1878, the forty-year-old Smith married twenty-one-year-old Mary A.
Knox of Philadelphia. Little is known about Mary Knox Smith, or how
she and Tom met, but they had a long marriage. The ceremony was performed at the Church of the Evangelists on Catherine Street in Philadelphia by the Rev. Thomas L. Franklin. It was the first marriage for both. They
had three children: Manon Virginia Smith, born July 4, 1880; Thomas Wilt-
berger Smith, born September 12, 1882; and Robert Morris Smith (evidently
named for the second commander of the 6th Pennsylvania Cavalry), born
June 4, 1887.[8]

In 1891, Smith applied for a soldier's pension. The application stated that
he suffered from severe rheumatism and heart problems. Smith wrote,
"The first recollection I have of suffering with Rheumatism is about the 2nd
year of my enlistment or about the latter part of 1862 and from that on to the
present time. I had it in different parts at different times in my legs, arms,
back, shoulders, chest, stomach and it has affected my heart very much
since I came out of the Army." The application was supported by affidavits
from both friends and Smith's treating physician, who noted that Smith suffered from valvular trouble and hypertrophy of the heart, and also that "he
is never well. The rheumatism he has all of the time."[9] At the end of his application, Smith wrote: "I have often been advised by my Friends to apply for
a Pension ever since I came out of the Army but I have always felt backward

about doing so as long as I could make a living for myself but now that I have become almost a helpless cripple from Rheumatism which I contracted in the service I am compelled to ask for a pension."[10] By the time Smith applied for a pension, the family's only source of income was whatever money Mary Knox Smith could earn by doing physical labor.[11]

The application was initially denied by the pension commissioner on the grounds that it did not demonstrate disability to a pensionable degree, and that there was insufficient evidence to show that the illness resulted from service. Finally, a pension of eight dollars per month was approved in 1896, just before Smith's death.[12] Despite the determination that he was not disabled, Smith apparently never was able to support himself from the 1870s on.

Evidently, rheumatism was not the only problem that plagued Tom Smith. Always fond of the taste of whiskey, Smith became an alcoholic in later years. He died on April 26, 1896, of chronic alcoholism. A small funeral was held at the family home at 2 P.M. on Saturday, May 2, 1896, with "relatives and friends invited to attend."[13] No mention of his old comrades in arms or his own military service was made in the brief obituary. Following the funeral, Thomas W. Smith was buried in Monument Cemetery in Philadelphia, ending the long and fascinating story of one man's service in the Army of the Potomac.[14] He was only fifty-eight years old.

Smith apparently did not participate in Civil War veterans' events. Perhaps he was bitter that his service had destroyed his health, or perhaps he simply did not care. Regardless of the cause, Smith does not seem to have kept in touch with his former comrades in arms.

While he was not a highly educated man, Thomas W. Smith's letters demonstrate a rare insight into the realities of service in the Army of the Potomac, and into army politics in that most political of wars. It is unfortunate that more of his letters did not survive or that he never took the time to write memoirs of his experiences, for the record of both his life and his service to his country remains incomplete. Nevertheless, his letters provide poignant insight into daily life in the Union cavalry during the Civil War, reflecting both a dedication to preserving a Union threatened from within and a young man's experiences in the greatest adventure of his life.

Appendixes

A. Engagements of the 6th Pennsylvania Cavalry

The 6th Pennsylvania Cavalry was known by "Rush's Lancers," its nickname or local designation. Like almost all Civil War units, the regiment was also known by an alternate designation derived from the name of its commanding officer. Names of this type used by or for the regiment are shown below in order of command:

> Richard H. Rush's cavalry
> Charles L. Leiper's cavalry
> John H. McArthur's cavalry
> C. Ross Smith's cavalry
> Albert P. Morrow's cavalry
> Robert Morris, Jr.'s cavalry
> John H. Gardner's cavalry
> George H. Clymer's cavalry
> Henry C. Whelan's cavalry
> J. Henry Hazeltine's cavalry
> William P. C. Treichel's cavalry
> James Starr's cavalry
> Abraham D. Price's cavalry
> Charles B. Coxe's cavalry
> Bernard H. Harkness's cavalry

On December 10, 1861, the 6th Pennsylvania Cavalry was ordered to Washington, D.C., where it joined the Army of the Potomac. On provost duty until the following May, it remained with the Army of the Potomac until August 1864. It then joined the Army of the Shenandoah, returning to service in November 1864 for the remainder of its career. Listed below are the specific higher command assignments of the 6th Pennsylvania Cavalry.

TABLE 1. LOCATION AND DATES OF ENGAGEMENTS

UNIT ASSIGNED	DATES OF SERVICE
Emory's Brigade, Cooke's Cavalry Division, Cavalry Reserve, Army of the Potomac	December 1861–July 1862
Emory's Second Brigade, Cavalry Division, Army of the Potomac	July 1862–August 1862
Third Brigade, Pleasonton's Cavalry Division, Army of the Potomac	July 1862–November 1862
Headquarters, Left Grand Division, Army of the Potomac	November 1862–Feburary 1863
Reserve Brigade, Cavalry Corps, Army of the Potomac	February 1863–June 1863
Reserve Brigade, First Division, Cavalry Corps, Army of the Potomac	June 1863–August 1864
Third (Reserve) Brigade, First Cavalry Division, Cavalry Corps, Army of the Shenandoah	August 1864–November 1864
Third (Reserve) Brigade, First Cavalry Division, Cavalry Corps, Army of the Potomac	November 1864–June 1865

TABLE 2. ELEMENTS INVOLVED IN ENGAGEMENTS

ENGAGEMENT	DATE
Scout to Hunter's Mills, Va.	March 19, 1862
Advance from Fortress Monroe to Yorktown, Va.	May 3–5, 1862
Reconnaissance to New Castle and Hanovertown, Ferry, Va.	May 22, 1862
Reconnaissance to Hanover Court House, Va.	May 24, 1862
Skirmish, Hanover Court House, Va. (Co. C)	May 25, 1862
Operations about Hanover Court House, Va.	May 27–29, 1862
Skirmish, Hanover Court House, Va. (Co. A)	May 27, 1862

TABLE 2. ELEMENTS INVOLVED IN ENGAGEMENTS (CONT.)

ENGAGEMENT	DATE
Occupation, Ashland, Va.	May 30, 1862
Reconnaissance to Hanover Court House, Va.	June 10–12, 1862
Operations against Stuart's Raid about White House, Va.	June 12–15, 1862
Skirmish, Garlick's Landing, Pamunkey River, Va.	June 13, 1862
Seven Days Battles, Va.	June 25–July 1, 1862
Affair, Beaver Dam Station, Va. (Cos. B, C, G, H)	June 26, 1862
Battles, Gaines' Mill, Cold Harbor, Chickahominy, Va.	June 27, 1862
Battle, Glendale, Frazier's Farm, Charles City Crossroads, New Market Crossroads, Willis Church, Va.	June 30, 1862
Battle, Malvern Hill, Crew's Farm, Va. (Co. F)	July 1, 1862
Skirmishes, Falls Church, Va.	September 2–4, 1862
Maryland campaign	September 6–22, 1862
Skirmish, South Mountain, Md.	September 13, 1862
Skirmish, Jefferson, Md.	September 13, 1862
Battle, Crampton's Gap, South Mountain, Md. (Cos. B, G, I)	September 14, 1862
Battle, Antietam, Sharpsburg, Md. (Cos. B, G, I)	September 16–17, 1862
Action, Sharpsburg, Shepherdstown, and Blackford's Ford (Boteler's Ford) and Williamsport, Md.	September 19, 1862
Operations in Loudoun, Fauquier, and Rappahannock counties, Va.	October 26– November 10, 1862
Actions, Bloomfield and Upperville, Va.	November 2–3, 1862
Battle, Fredericksburg, Va.	December 12–15, 1862

TABLE 2. ELEMENTS INVOLVED IN ENGAGEMENTS (CONT.)

ENGAGEMENT	DATE
Skirmish, Occoquan River, Va. (Cos. B, G)	December 19, 1862
Burnside's "Mud March," Va. (Cos. A, D, E)	January 20–24, 1863
Chancellorsville campaign	April 27–May 6, 1863
Stoneman's Raid, Va. (Co. L)	April 29–May 8, 1863
Skirmish, Raccoon Ford, Va. (detachment)	April 30, 1863
Engagement, Brandy Station and Beverly Ford, Va.	June 9, 1863
Reconnaissance to Ashby's Gap, Va. (Co. A)	June 14, 1863
Gettysburg campaign	June 9–July 24, 1863
Skirmish, Greencastle, Pa.	June 20, 1863
Battle, Gettysburg, Pa.	July 1–3, 1863
Action, Williamsport, Md.	July 6, 1863
Action, Boonsborough, Md.	July 8, 1863
Skrimishes at and near Funkstown, Md.	July 10–13, 1863
Skirmish, Aldie, Va. (detachment)	July 11, 1863
Skirmishes, Kelly's Ford, Va.	July 31–August 1, 1863
Action, Brandy Station, Va.	August 1, 1863
Advance from the Rappahannock to the Rapidan, Va.	September 13–17, 1863
Bristoe campaign	October 9–22, 1863
Skirmish, Manassas Junction, Va.	October 17, 1863
Skirmish, Bristoe Station, Kettle Run, Va.	October 18, 1863
Advance to the line of the Rappahannock, Va.	November 7–8, 1863
Mine Run Campaign, Va.	November 26–December 2, 1863

TABLE 2. ELEMENTS INVOLVED IN ENGAGEMENTS (CONT.)

ENGAGEMENT	DATE
Demonstration on the Rapidan, Va.	February 5–7, 1864
Custer's Raid in Albemarle County, Va.	February 26– March 1, 1864
Skirmish near Charlottesville, Va.	February 29, 1864
Skirmish, Burton's Ford, Rapidan River, Va.	March 1, 1864
Skirmish, Stannardsville, Va.	March 1, 1864
Wilderness campaign	May 4–June 12, 1864
Engagement, Todd's Tavern, Va.	May 7–8, 1864
Sheridan's Raid from Todd's Tavern to the James River, Va.	May 9–24, 1864
Engagement, Ground Squirrel Church, South Anna River, and Yellow Tavern, Richmond, Va. (separate detachments involved in separate actions)	May 11, 1864
Engagement, Meadow Bridge, Chickahominy River, Va.	May 12, 1864
Combat, Mechanicsville, Va.	May 12, 1864
Operations on the line of the Pamunkey River, Va.	May 26–28, 1864
Action, Hanovertown, Pamunkey River, Va.	May 27, 1864
Skirmish, Hanovertown Ferry, Va.	May 27, 1864
Operations on the line of the Totopotomoy River, Va.	May 28–31, 1864
Engagement, Old Church, Va.	May 30, 1864
Action, Mattadequin Creek, Va.	May 30, 1864
Combat, Bethesda Church, Va.	May 31–June 1, 1864
Engagement, Cold Harbor, Va.	May 31–June 1, 1864

TABLE 2. ELEMENTS INVOLVED IN ENGAGEMENTS (CONT.)

ENGAGEMENT	DATE
Skirmish, McClellan's Bridge, Va.	June 2, 1864
Skirmishes, Haw's Shop, Va.	June 4–5, 1864
Sheridan's Trevilian Raid, Va.	June 7–24, 1864
Engagement, Trevilian Station, Central R.R., Va.	June 11–12, 1864
Action, Newark (Mallory's Cross Roads), Va.	June 12, 1864
Action, Black River (Tunstall's Station) and White House (St. Peter's Church), Va.	June 21, 1864
Action, Jones' Bridge, Va.	June 23, 1864
Siege operations against Petersburg and Richmond, Va.	July 4–30, 1864
Demonstration on the North Side of the James River and Engagements at Deep Bottom (Darbytown), Strawberry Plains, and New Market Road, Va.	July 27–29, 1864
Engagement, Charles City Cross Roads, Va.	July 27–28, 1864
Engagement, Malvern Hill, Va.	July 28, 1864
Sheridan's campaign in the Shenandoah Valley, Va.	August 7– November 28, 1864
Action near Stone Chapel, Va.	August 10, 1864
Action, Toll Gate near White Post, Va.	August 11, 1864
Action near Newtown, Va.	August 11, 1864
Skirmish near Strasburg, Va.	August 14, 1864
Skirmish, Summit Point, W. Va.	August 21, 1864
Skirmish, Summit Point, W. Va.	August 23–24, 1864
Action near Keraneysville, W. Va.	August 25, 1864
Skirmishes, Leetown and Smithfield, W. Va.	August 28, 1864

TABLE 2. ELEMENTS INVOLVED IN ENGAGEMENTS (CONT.)

ENGAGEMENT	DATE
Engagement, Smithfield, Crossing of the Opequon, W. Va.	August 29, 1864
Sheridan's Expedition from Winchester, Va.	February 27–March 25, 1865
Engagement, Waynesborough, Va.	March 2, 1865
Appomattox campaign, Va.	March 28–April 9, 1865
Skirmishes on the line of Hatcher's and Gravelly Runs, Va.	March 30, 1865
Engagement, Dinwiddie Court House, Va.	March 30–31, 1865
Battle, Five Forks, Va.	April 1, 1865
Action, Scott's Cross Roads, Va.	April 2, 1865
Skirmish, Tabernacle Church (Beaver Dam Creek), Va.	April 4, 1865
Engagement, Sailor's Creek, Va.	April 6, 1865
Engagement, Appomattox Station, Va.	April 8, 1865
Engagement, Clover Hill, Appomattox Court House, Va.	April 9, 1865
Surrender, Appomattox Court House, Va.	April 9, 1865
Expedition from Burkesville and Petersburg to Danville and South Boston, Va.	April 23–29, 1865

On May 2, 1865, the regiment was ordered from Danville to Washington where it took part in the Grand Review of Eastern Armies held on May 23. The regiment was consolidated with the 1st and 17th Pennsylvania Cavalry Regiments on June 17, 1865, to form the 2d Pennsylvania Provisional Cavalry. Moved to Louisville and Lebanon, Kentucky, a short time later, the regiment was mustered out of Federal service at Lebanon on August 7, 1865.

During its career, the 6th Pennsylvania Cavalry sustained the loss of seven officers and seventy-one enlisted men killed or mortally wounded. An additional three officers and eighty-six enlisted men died from disease or other nonbattlefield causes.

The Congressional Medal of Honor was awarded to Capt. Frank Furness for his actions at Trevilian Station, Virginia, on June 12, 1864, when he "voluntarily carried a box of ammunition across an open field swept by the enemy's fire to the relief of an outpost whose ammunition had been almost exhausted, but which was thus able to hold its important position . . . ."

B. A CHRONOLOGICAL LISTING OF THE LETTERS OF SGT. THOMAS W. SMITH

1862

January 7 to Dear Sister
January 15 to Joseph W. Smith
January 26 to Dear Mother
January 26 to Joseph W. Smith
February 1 to Joseph W. Smith
February 14 to Joseph W. Smith
February 15 to Joseph W. Smith
February 28 to Joseph W. Smith
March 16 to Joseph W. Smith
March 20 to Joseph W. Smith
March 27 to Dear Mother
April 8 to Dear Father
April 8 to Dear Sister (incomplete letter)
Undated, but early May to Joseph W. Smith
May 7 to Susan Smith
May 15 to Dear Sister
May 20 to Susan Smith
May 25 to Joseph W. Smith
May 28 to Joseph W. Smith
Undated, but in mid June to Susan Smith
June 17 to Jane Smith
June 20 to Dear Father
July 9 to Joseph W. Smith

July 25 to Dear Sister
August 7 to Joseph W. Smith
August 23 to Dear Sister
September 6 to Joseph W. Smith
September 11 to Joseph W. Smith
October 4 to Dear Sister
October 8 to Joseph W. Smith
October 15 to Dear Father
October 18 to Dear Sister
October 23 to Dear Sister
October 31 to Dear Sister (presumably Jane)
November 21 to Joseph W. Smith
November 30 to Ben Smith
December 4 to Jane Smith
December 10 to Joseph W. Smith
December 29 to Dear Sister

1863

January 7 to Dear Sister
January 14 to Joseph W. Smith
April 4 to Joseph W. Smith
April 10 to Joseph W. Smith
April 16 to Joseph W. Smith
April 24 to Joseph W. Smith
April 29 to Joseph W. Smith
May 8 to Joseph W. Smith
May 22 to Joseph W. Smith
June 2 to Joseph W. Smith
June 8 to Joseph W. Smith
June 15 to Joseph W. Smith
June 27 to Dear Sister
June 28 fragment of diary
July 11 to Susan Smith
July 28 to Joseph W. Smith
August 5 to Joseph W. Smith
August 10 to Joseph W. Smith
September 2 to Joseph W. Smith

November 1 to Joseph W. Smith
December 13 to Joseph W. Smith
December 16 to Joseph W. Smith

1864

March 3 to Joseph W. Smith
April 5 to Jane Smith
May 3 to Dear Sister
June 3 to Dear Sister
June 27 to Susan Smith
July 13 to Susan Smith

Total: 67 letters

Notes

INTRODUCTION

1. Frank H. Taylor, *Philadelphia in the Civil War* (Philadelphia, 1879), 48–184.

2. *Philadelphia Inquirer*, Nov. 8, 1864.

3. William H. Egle, ed., *Andrew Gregg Curtin: His Life and Services* (Philadelphia: Avil Printing, 1895), 417–20.

4. John C. Waugh, *Class of 1846* (New York: Warner, 1994), xiv–xvi.

5. Taylor, *Philadelphia in the Civil War*, 162.

6. George Archibald McCall to Peter McCall, May 27, 1861, Cadwalader Collection, Miscellaneous Box, Collection No. 1454, Historical Society of Pennsylvania, Philadelphia.

7. Joseph Blaschek, "The Story of Rush's Lancers," *National Tribune*, June 24, 1897.

8. Richard H. Rush service records, entry for Oct.–Nov. 1861, National Archives (NA), Washington, D.C.; Stephen Z. Starr, *The Union Cavalry in the Civil War*, 3 vols. (Baton Rouge: Louisiana State Univ. Press, 1974), 1:102.

9. George Meade, *The Life and Letters of George Gordon Meade*, 2 vols. (New York: Charles Scribner's Sons, 1913), 1:xv–1.

10. Blaschek, "The Story of Rush's Lancers."

11. Ibid.; T. F. Thiele, "The Evolution of Cavalry in the American Civil War, 1861–1865" (Ph.D. diss., University of Michigan, 1951), 76; Col. Alexander Biddle to Dear Julia, Oct. 22, 1862, Rush/Williams/Biddle Family Papers, series IV: Biddle Family, box 30, Rosenbach Museum, Philadelphia.

12. Robert F. O'Neill, Jr., "The Federal Cavalry on the Peninsula" (unpublished manuscript, 1997), 9; *The War of the Rebellion: A Compilation of the Official Records of the Union and Confederate Armies*, 128 vols. (Washington, D.C.: GPO, 1880–1901), ser. 3, vol. 1:622 (hereafter cited as *OR*, with all references to series 1 unless otherwise stated).

13. 1860 Census for the Ninth Precinct of Philadelphia, RG M653, reel no. 1159, 249.

14. Thomas W. Smith Pension File, NA.

15. Taylor, *Philadelphia in the Civil War*, 303; Samuel P. Bates, *History of Pennsylvania Volunteers, 1861–1865*, 3 vols. (Harrisburg, Pa: B. Singerly, 1869), 8:775–76; Thomas W. Smith service records, RG 94, NA; James A. Congdon, *Congdon's Cavalry Compendium: Containing Instructions for Non-Commissioned Officers and Privates in the Cavalry Service* (Philadelphia: J. B. Lippincott, 1864), 58.

16. Samuel L. Gracey, *Annals of the Sixth Pennsylvania Cavalry* (1868; reprint, Lancaster, Ohio: VanBerg, 1996), 23, 26–27. Gracey was the regimental chaplain. Born in Philadelphia in 1835 and educated at Boston University, Gracey served throughout the war, acting as pastor for several different congregations after the end of hostilities in 1865. In 1890 he was appointed consul to China, a post he held until 1897. He died at home in Boston in 1911 and

was brought to rest in Philadelphia. He lies under a simple headstone that reads "Soldier-Clergyman-Diplomat."

17. Sydney L. Wright Memoir, Wright Family Papers, Collection No. 2096, William Redwood Wright Section Folder, Historical Society of Pennsylvania; OR, ser. 3, vol. 1:606.

18. Theodore Sage to Dear Sister, Dec. 24, 1861, Harrisburg Civil War Roundtable Collection, U.S. Army Military History Institute (USAMHI), Carlisle Barracks, Pennsylvania.

19. Smith's service records, NA.

1. "WE DRILL FROM MORNING TO NIGHT NOW"

1. Gracey, Annals, 38. The regiment paraded through the streets of Washington on January 7, the day before Smith wrote this letter to his sister. Ill for much of the winter that year, McClellan was often unable to perform his duties.

2. The army had a poor system for paying its soldiers, who received only about thirteen dollars per month. Soldiers often had to wait months to get paid, causing the men great hardship.

3. Gracey, Annals, 38. Company B was detailed to provost duty in Washington, D.C., on January 8, and Company A was sent the following day. The two companies were to alternate days; they were relieved after two weeks of service in this capacity.

4. Philadelphia Inquirer, Feb. 1, 1862; Capt. Robert Milligan to Dear Levi, Jan. 15, 1862, Sue Clark Knight Papers, Wisconsin State Archives, Madison.

5. Smith refers to his youngest sibling, Ben.

6. Shelby Foote, The Civil War: A Narrative, 3 vols. (New York: Vintage Books, 1986), 1:242.

7. Pvt. Samuel Boyer of Philadelphia, also a member of Company I. Bates, History 2:775.

8. The soldier to whom Smith refers is Albert Payson Morrow, who was captured by the Confederates in June 1862. After being exchanged, he was again captured during the May 1863 Stoneman Raid and again exchanged. Commissioned an officer in late 1862, he was wounded during Ulric Dahlgren's raid after the Battle of Gettysburg. Young Morrow drew the attention of Brig. Gen. John Buford, who appointed Morrow to his staff in July 1863. Morrow served in this capacity until Buford's death in December 1863; he then returned to field service with the Lancers. By the end of the Civil War, he had achieved the rank of lieutenant colonel of the regiment and went on to a long and distinguished career in the Regular Army after the Civil War. Ultimately achieving the rank of colonel, Morrow became famous as an Indian fighter. See "Record of Colonel Albert P. Morrow," Wright Family Papers.

9. Pvt. Granville S. P. Arnold, age eighteen, a coachmaker from East Coventry, Pennsylvania, was a member of Smith's Company I. Arnold died at Camp Barclay on January 30, 1862. Douglas Harper, comp., "Index of Civil War Soldiers and Sailors from Chester County, Pennsylvania," Chester County Historical Society, Chester, Pennsylvania.

10. Philadelphia Inquirer, Feb. 1, 1862; Capt. Robert Milligan to Dear Levi, Feb. 8, 1862, Sue Clark Knight Papers.

11. Captain James Starr, commanding Company I. Starr, a lawyer by training, had come from the First City Troop. By the end of the war, he proved himself a brave and capable leader of men. James Starr pension file, RG 15, NA.

12. Smith often refers to hail in his letters. Given the time of year, it is clear that he confuses sleet and hail, as he does here.

13. Chaplain Gracey described the sword and the ceremony where it was presented: "On Thursday, the 6th, the monotony of camp life was varied by the interesting ceremony of a sword presentation to Colonel Rush, by the non-commissioned officers of the regiment. The sword was one of the finest of Philadelphia workmanship, and was richly ornamented on the blade with beautiful designs and mottoes of sterling patriotism. The grip is of solid silver, bound with gold lace, and the initials 'R. H. R.' in raised silver, with the inscription, 'Presented to Colonel Richard H. Rush, of the Philadelphia Light Cavalry, by the noncommissioned officers of the regiment.' The men presenting the weapon formed on the parade ground, and marched to the Colonel's headquarters, preceded by the regimental band. On arriving there, the regimental Sergeant-Major, Eugene P. Bertrand, made a neat presentation speech. The Colonel replied in his usual happy manner. After music by the band, other officers were called upon, and short speeches were made by Lieutenant-Colonel [John H.] McArthur and Majors [C. Ross] Smith and [Robert] Morris [Jr.]." Gracey, Annals, 38–39.

14. Sgt. Archer Mavis of Philadelphia was later commissioned an officer.

15. Capt. Robert Milligan to Dear Levi, Feb. 8, 1862, Sue Clark Knight Papers.

16. Smith refers to the Potomac River, the dividing line between Washington and the Confederacy.

17. Gracey, Annals, 39–40.

18. By this point in the war, McClellan was typically still assigned fragments of volunteer cavalry regiments to various infantry brigades for use as couriers and sometimes as scouts. Only the Regular Cavalry served in a cohesive unit. Camp Casey refers to Gen. Silas Casey's camp, also located in the District of Columbia.

19. This was a Philadelphia newspaper of the time that was evidently very popular among the members of the regiment.

20. Smith is referring to 1st Lt. Oswald Jackson of Philadelphia and Maj. Gen. Erasmus D. Keyes, who was commanding a corps in the Army of the Potomac.

21. Gracey, Annals, 40.

22. Ibid., 41.

23. Evidently, the men did not believe that Federal greenbacks would have value on the Virginia Peninsula. Instead, they gave up their paper money for specie, which was more negotiable.

24. Gracey, Annals, 41.

25. Fortress Monroe was a major Federal installation charged with protecting the entrance to the important shipyard at Hampton Roads, Virginia, near Norfolk. Saddler Dorastus McCord of Company E described I as "a beautiful fort." Dorastus McCord to Dear Sister, Apr. 7, 1862, Spanish-American War Survey, Civil War Box, USAMHI. McCord was killed in action at the Battle of Todd's Tavern on May 7, 1864. McCord service records, NA.

26. The Monitor, the Union's first ironclad warship, was designed by a Swede named John Ericsson and brought to Hampton to protect the harbor.

27. Emlen N. Carpenter to Dear Mr. Henszey, June 20, 1862, Alexander R. Chamberlin Collection, USAMHI; *OR*, vol. 11, 3:36.

28. Benjamin W. Crowninshield, "Sheridan at Winchester," *Atlantic Monthly* 42 (1878), 684; Ezra J. Warner, *Generals in Blue* (Baton Rouge: Louisiana State Univ. Press, 1964), 142–43; O'Neill, "The Federal Cavalry," 49.

29. Maj. Gen. John B. Magruder, the district commander, burned the town after hearing rumors that it would be seized and converted into a camp for freed slaves. He did not want to see the historic town desecrated. Stephen W. Sears, *To the Gates of Richmond: The Peninsula Campaign* (New York: Ticknor and Fields, 1992).

30. The *Merrimack* was a United States Navy warship that was burned and scuttled when the Union forces abandoned Grosport Navy Yard in Norfolk in 1861. The Confederate navy raised it and rebuilt it as America's first ironclad warship. Armed with ten cannon and an iron ram on the bow, the *Merrimack*, renamed the C.S.S. *Virginia*, was greatly feared by the Union navy, which sent the *Monitor* to Hampton in an effort to counter its threat. Foote, *The Civil War* 1:255–56.

31. Smith refers to Maj. Gen. Ulysses S. Grant's victory at the Battle of Shiloh, Tennessee, fought on April 5 and 6, 1862.

32. In the opening engagement of McClellan's Peninsula campaign, after an extremely cautious advance, McClellan captured the Revolutionary War battlefield and town of Yorktown. His advance was checked by a small force under Magruder's command. The cautious McClellan could have steamrolled over the small Confederate force, but instead he chose to besiege the town, and finally, after a nearly fourteen-day delay, he captured the town. It was a victory, but a dubious one at best.

2. "We Have Had Quite Stirring Times about Here"

1. Brig. Gen. George Stoneman, West Point class of 1846. A classmate of both George McClellan and Thomas J. "Stonewall" Jackson, Stoneman was a Regular who had spent his entire career in the mounted arm. Stoneman served as McClellan's first chief of cavalry and held this purely administrative position during the Peninsula campaign. He later commanded a division of infantry. In the spring of 1863, when the Army of the Potomac's cavalry was consolidated into a cohesive corps, Stoneman was its first commander. He was the first chief of the Cavalry Bureau in the fall of 1863 and later commanded the Army of the Ohio's Cavalry Corps during the 1864 Atlanta campaign. Warner, *Generals in Blue*, 481–82.

2. While Smith does not identify the general, it is probably Stoneman, who had a crusty nature. The duties of the chief of cavalry included responsibility for all of the horses of the Army of the Potomac, would have fallen under Stoneman's jurisdiction.

3. This comment is a good reflection of the tension between the classes within the regiment.

4. Gracey, *Annals*, 42.

5. The "brigadier general" was Col. George A. H. Blake of the 1st U.S. Cavalry, and the brigade commander was Col. David McMurtrie Gregg, a first cousin of Pennsylvania gov-

ernor Andrew Gregg Curtin. Gregg, an extremely competent cavalry officer, went on to command a division of the Army of the Potomac's Cavalry Corps during 1863 and 1864. His younger brother Thomas was a lieutenant in the Lancers.

6. Unable to identify.

7. Charles Malsperger of Philadelphia.

8. Capt. James Starr, commander of Company I.

9. Abraham D. Price of Philadelphia. Price was later commissioned an officer and held the rank of major by the end of the war.

10. John P. Kepner of Philadelphia. Kepner was reduced in rank to private shortly after the end of the Peninsula campaign. In 1864 he was discharged from the Lancers so he could reenlist as a hospital steward. Kepner service records, NA.

11. Sgt. Richard C. Finn of Philadelphia.

12. Sgt. Lawrence C. Pennington of Philadelphia, killed at the Battle of Trevilian Station, Virginia, on June 11, 1864. Bates, *History*, 775.

13. Sgt. Michael Towers of Philadelphia was later promoted to second lieutenant after reenlisting in 1864. Bates, *History*, 775.

14. Edward McGratton of Philadelphia was later busted to the rank of private and discharged as a private at the end of his term of enlistment in the fall of 1864.

15. Samuel Wright of Philadelphia, who was wounded in action on March 1, 1863, but served out the term of his enlistment. Bates, *History*, 775.

16. James Boone of Philadelphia.

17. William Wilhour of Philadelphia.

18. James Keller of Philadelphia. Keller was promoted to captain after his reenlistment, serving with Company I of the 2d Provisional Pennsylvania Cavalry, a veteran regiment formed after the Confederate surrender at Appomattox. Bates, *History*, 776.

19. Robert Hamilton of Philadelphia. Evidently, Smith's assessment of Hamilton was correct, because he is listed on the muster roll as a private, which indicates that Hamilton, like McGratton, was later busted back to private for the duration of his term of enlistment. Ibid., 776.

20. Patrick Cardiff of Philadelphia, who later deserted. Ibid., 775.

21. Samuel Roberts of Philadelphia, who only enlisted on February 5, 1862, well after most of the other members of Company I. Roberts was a prisoner of war from August 13, 1864, until February 23, 1865. He was discharged in March 1865, just after his release. Ibid., 776.

22. Alexander Biddle to Julia Biddle, Jan. 19, 1863, Rush/Williams/Biddle Family Papers.

23. Gracey, *Annals*, 43.

24. The torpedoes that Smith describes are known today as land mines.

25. One of the first battlefield monuments erected in the United States.

26. Gracey, *Annals*, 44. Specifically, this was the home of Gen. Robert E. Lee's son, Brig. Gen. William H. F. "Rooney" Lee, as well as the place where George Washington courted Rooney Lee's grandmother, Martha Custis.

27. Robert Milligan to Dear Sir, May 17, 1862, Sue Clark Knight Papers.

28. The actual name of this town is Barhamsville.

29. Brig. Gen. Philip St. George Cooke, commanding the Cavalry Reserve.

30. Bowie knives.

31. McClellan believed that a Rebel host of more than two hundred thousand men faced him at Yorktown, when only about fifteen thousand men actually manned the Southern lines. Hence, McClellan ordered the siege of the Confederate fortifications there. After a month-long siege, Maj. Gen. John B. Magruder, evacuated the town the night before McClellan had ordered a grand assault by the Army of the Potomac. This was the cause of the haste referred to in Smith's letter. Sears, *To the Gates of Richmond*, 60–62.

32. Again, this is probably a reference to Barhamsville.

33. Milligan to Dear Sir, May 17, 1862, Sue Clark Knight Papers. Milligan resigned from the regiment in January 1863 on a Surgeon's Certificate of Disability, resulting from illness contracted in the field. Milligan service records, NA.

34. Gracey, *Annals*, 44.

35. Richard Rush to Col. Tyler, May 23, 1862, Lewis Leigh Collection, USAMHI.

36. Memorandum of Col. Richard H. Rush, May 31, 1862, Frank Moore, ed., *Rebellion Record: A Diary of American Events with Documents, Narratives, Illustrative Incidents, Poetry, Etc.*, 11 vols. and supp. (New York, 1861–68), 5:158–59; Lt. Theodore Sage to Dear Parents, May 24, 1862, Harrisburg Civil War Roundtable Collection.

37. Old Church is northeast of Richmond, between Tunstall's Station and Hanover Court House. J. E. B. Stuart's raid passed through Old Church on its way to Tunstall's Station.

38. The Lancers actually uncovered the presence of a strong Confederate force located near Hanover Court House, Virginia, not far from Richmond. On May 23, after this information was reported to Maj. Gen. Fitz John Porter, commander of the Federal Fifth Corps, Porter sent a strong force of cavalry, infantry, and artillery to confront the Confederates in the Fifth Corps's first combat. The small force commanded by Col. Gouverneur K. Warren of the 5th New York Infantry, which included the Lancers, joined this column.

39. Actually, the Lancers accompanied the entire Fifth Corps on its advance toward the large Confederate force awaiting them at Hanover Court House.

40. Gracey, *Annals*, 45.

41. OR, vol. 11, 1:668. This was a ferry across the Pamunkey River, northeast of the town of Hanover Court House. Sears, *Gates of Richmond*, 116.

42. By gum coats, Smith means the rubber ponchos issued to the men of the Army of the Potomac.

43. Smith is apparently referring to Lt. Edwin L. Tevis of Company C, although this cannot be confirmed.

44. The mission of the combined force of infantry, artillery, and cavalry was to capture and destroy a bridge over the Pamunkey River, far behind the Confederate main battle line. This force was commanded by Col. Gouverneur K. Warren.

45. Pvt. Samuel Boyer of Company I.

46. Lt. Frank H. Furness of Company I, Philadelphia. Furness won the Medal of Honor at the 1864 Battle of Trevilian Station.

47. Porter ordered the force under Warren to pursue the enemy to the east of the town and to destroy the wagon bridge across the Pamunkey. The Lancers led the way and captured a company of the 28th North Carolina Infantry in the process. OR, vol. 12, 1:736.

48. The number of casualties reported by Gen. Fitz John Porter, commanding the expedition to Hanover Court House, was 355. Ibid., 685.

49. Given this success, it really is something of a mystery why McClellan did not plan and execute more operations of a similar nature. If the first was successful, there were good prospects for future success for other combined force operations of this nature, but this appears to be the only time that McClellan ordered such an action; OR, vol. 12, 1:683; Sidney Morris Davis, *Common Soldier, Uncommon War: Life as a Civil War Cavalryman*, ed. Charles F. Cooney (Bethesda, Md.: SMD Group, 1994), 148.

50. OR, vol. 12, 1:736; Gracey, *Annals*, 46.

51. Richard H. Rush to Gov. Andrew G. Curtin, May 31, 1862, quoted in Gracey, *Annals*, 47.

52. The force Smith described here is the combined force commanded by Colonel Warren.

53. These men belonged to the 4th Virginia Cavalry. Rush to Curtin, May 31, 1862, Lewis Leigh Collection.

54. Ibid.; Memorandum of Richard H. Rush, May 31, 1862, Lewis Leigh Collection; Statement of Col. Richard H. Rush, June 3, 1862, NA.

55. Interestingly, most of the regiment was originally mounted on solid little Morgan horses from Vermont. C. M. Ruff to Montgomery Meigs, Aug. 21, 1861, RG 839, file 194–95, NA.

56. A piece of paper money of small face value, especially one issued by some private banks or the U.S. government between 1862 and 1878. *Webster's New World Dictionary*, 14th ed., s.v. *plaster*.

57. Alexander Biddle to Julia Biddle, Jan. 17, 1863, Rush/Williams/Biddle Family Papers.

58. Emlen N. Carpenter to Dear Mr. Henszey, June 20, 1862, Alex R.Chamberlain Collection.

59. Smith refers to White House Landing on the James River, which served as McClellan's principal supply depot.

60. Smith refers to the pursuit of Stuart's raid here.

61. Capt. William Bedford Royall of the 5th U.S. Cavalry. Francis E. Heitman, *Historical Register and Dictionary of the U.S. Army*, 2 vols. (Washington, D.C.: GPO, 1904), 1:849.

62. Lt. Albert P. Morrow of Philadelphia and Lt. Charles E. Davis of Company E.

63. Horstmann Brothers and Co. was a large military supply house located at the intersection of Fifth and Cherry Streets in downtown Philadelphia.

64. OR, vol. 11, 1:1017.

65. See Smith's service records, NA.

66. Congdon, *Congdon's Cavalry Compendium*, 57.

67. Brig. Gen. George A. McCall of the Pennsylvania Reserve Division of Porter's Fifth Corps. Mechanicsville was a small town north of Richmond became integral to the coming Seven Days Battles, the culmination of the Peninsula campaign.

68. Professor Thadeus Lowe brought gas balloons to the Army of the Potomac. These balloons were used for observation purposes. They were used to scout and watch the movements of the Confederates. They were viewed as a great novelty by both sides.

69. The 1st Pennsylvania Reserves of McCall's Division of Pennsylvania Reserves, assigned to the Fifth Corps.

70. Lt. Col. Abraham K. Arnold, "The Cavalry at Gaines' Mill," *Journal of the United States Cavalry Association* 2 (1889): 358–59.

71. OR, vol. 51, 1:716–17.

72. Maj. Gen. Ambrose E. Burnside, commander of the Federal Ninth Corps, recently victorious in a campaign to take the coastal area of North Carolina around New Berne. Burnside was a close friend and West Point classmate of McClellan.

73. In the 1880s Smith applied for a veteran's pension. The passage of this letter was submitted in support of his pension application and cited for the proposition that Smith's health problems, leading to the pension application, began with the ailment cited in this letter home.

74. *Philadelphia Press*, July 21, 1862.

75. Lt. Abraham D. Price of Company I, and Maj. Gen. Samuel P. Heintzelman of Pennsylvania, commanding the Army of the Potomac's Third Corps.

76. Gracey, *Annals*, 81.

77. Companies C and H of the 6th Pennsylvania were detached to serve as headquarters guards for Maj. Gen. Fitz John Porter, commander of the Fifth Corps. Maj. Gen. William B. Franklin served as commander of the Army of the Potomac's Sixth Corps.

78. Only two companies of Lancers attached to Porter's headquarters detail were sent to aid Maj. Gen. John Pope's Army of Virginia. Pope had fought a major battle with Stonewall Jackson at Cedar Mountain, in Culpeper County, Virginia, on August 9. Pope had nearly been destroyed by a clever trap set by Robert E. Lee and had withdrawn toward his supply depot at Manassas Junction, near the old Bull Run battlefield. Porter's Fifth Corps was ordered to go to Pope's aid, although McClellan seems to have dragged his feet in dispatching his favorite lieutenant to his rival Pope.

79. Robert, or Bob, appears to be a cousin of Tom, because it becomes clear in a later letter that his last name was also Smith. It is known that Bob enlisted in the 148th Pennsylvania Infantry, also known as the Corn Exchange Regiment.

80. Quoted in Gracey, *Annals*, 65.

3. "I Have Been Very Low with the Fever and Ague"

1. OR, vol. 19, 1:180; Gracey, *Annals*, 87.

2. Smith refers to the Long Bridge over the Potomac River, one of the major routes of transport from northern Virginia into the District of Columbia.

3. The 114th Pennsylvania Volunteer Infantry, commanded by Col. Charles H. T. Collis, who later won the Medal of Honor at the Battle of Fredericksburg. Collis's Zouaves were also a Philadelphia regiment.

4. The 118th Pennsylvania Volunteer Infantry, commanded by Col. Charles M. Prevost, of the Fifth Army Corps. Another Philadelphia regiment it was made up of men who

worked in Philadelphia's commodities exchange. Tom's cousin Bob was a member of this regiment.

5. Maj. Gen. Ambrose E. Burnside's Ninth Army Corps, just off a triumphant campaign in the coastal region of North Carolina.

6. Joseph Janvier Woodward, *Outline of the Chief Camp Diseases of the United States Armies* (Philadelphia: J. B. Lippincott, 1863), 134, 80–82.

7. Clymer was one of the few officers of the regiment not from Philadelphia. A member of one of the most prominent families of Reading, Pennsylvania, Clymer had personally raised Company G in Reading. According to Gracey, Major Clymer was one of the most popular officers of the regiment.

8. Smith refers to Rockville, Maryland, about twenty miles from the center of the District of Columbia.

9. Maj. Gen. Darius N. Couch, commanding the First Division of the Fourth Army Corps, temporarily attached to Franklin's Sixth Corps.

10. Lt. Abraham D. Price of Company I.

11. Gracey, *Annals*, 90.

12. Robert Milligan to Dear Levi, Oct. 7, 1862, Sue Clark Knight Papers.

13. Ibid.

14. Gracey, *Annals*, 97.

15. Robert Milligan to Dear Levi, Oct. 7, 1862, Sue Clark Knight Papers.

16. Oliver Willets to Dear Sister, June 8, 1862, Richard Lewis Collection, Lexington, Va.

17. Smith refers to Strasburg, Pennsylvania, in Lancaster County, about thirty miles southeast of Harrisburg.

18. According to the *Official Records*, the 114th Pennsylvania was not involved in the Battle of Antietam.

19. Woodward, *Outline of Chief Camp Diseases*, 178–80.

20. Sgt. Richard C. Finn of Company I.

21. Charles E. Cadwalader to Richard H. Rush, Oct. 16, 1862, Cadwalader Collection.

22. *OR*, vol. 51, 1:41–42; Gracey, *Annals*, 111.

23. Identity unknown; however, these were probably women of the Christian Commission or one of the other mutual aid societies.

24. Gracey, *Annals*, 111, 113.

25. Smith seems to have invented a word here, combining "solemn" and "melancholy."

26. Neither of these men appears on the muster rolls of the regiment, so they must have been friends from home.

27. Thomas W. Smith pension file, NA; compiled service records of Sgt. Thomas W. Smith, NA.

4. "I Have Seen So Much, Heard So Much, and Been So Many Places"

1. Emlen N. Carpenter to Dear Mr. Henszey, Jan. 24, 1863, Alexander R. Chamberlain Collection.

2. *OR*, vol. 21:1004–5.

3. Ibid., vol. 25, 1:51.

4. Gracey, *Annals*, 128; Christian Geisel to Dear Sister, Mar. 10, 1863, Christian Geisel Letters, Pennsylvania State Archives, Harrisburg.

5. Aquia Creek, near Fredericksburg, Virginia.

6. Sibley tents were one of the primary camp tents used by the Union armies during the Civil War. They were large enough to hold ten men and their gear comfortably.

7. This was one of many reforms implemented by Hooker, such as creating distinctive corps badges for each infantry corps, intended to improve army morale. By and large, this strategy was remarkably effective.

8. Smith refers to Belle Plain Landing, located on the Rappahannock River near Falmouth.

9. Unidentified.

10. Here Smith refers to President Lincoln. He also, without directly saying so, expresses his disapproval of Lincoln's Emancipation Proclamation, issued on January 1, 1863.

11. Apr. 6, 1863, entry, Silas D. Wesson Diary, Civil War Times Illustrated Collection, USAMHI.

12. Alexander Biddle to Julia Biddle, Apr. 6, 1863, Rush/Williams/Biddle Family Papers.

13. *Philadelphia Inquirer*, Apr. 8, 1863.

14. Joseph Hooker to Samuel P. Bates, Apr. 2, 1878, Samuel P. Bates Papers, Pennsylvania State Archives, Harrisburg; OR, vol. 25, 1:1089, 1057.

15. A General Polerdi, first name unknown. W. P. Conrad and Ted Alexander, *When War Passed This Way* (Greencastle, Pa.: Lilian S. Besore Library, 1982), 117.

16. The Cavalry Corps actually left its winter camp on April 13, 1863.

17. There is no record of this fighting included in the *Official Records*. Smith probably refers to random skirmishing going on between pickets on either side of the river.

18. Smith was correct about Dougherty's intentions. The muster roll for the regiment indicates that Pvt. Joseph Dougherty of Company I deserted in April 1863. This was apparently a rumor.

19. Again, there is no reference to this in the *Official Records*. Presumably, Smith still refers to skirmishing.

20. Actually, the cavalry had no numeric designation. It was merely referred to as the Cavalry Corps.

21. United States Ford is another of the critical crossings of the Rappahannock River that saw much traffic during the course of the Civil War.

22. OR, vol. 25, 1:171.

23. Darius N. Couch, "The Chancellorsville Campaign," in *Battles and Leaders of the Civil War*, 4 vols., ed. Robert U. Johnson and Clarence C. Buel (New York: Century, 1884–1901), 3:161.

24. On the afternoon of May 1, the advance of Hooker's army collided with Jackson's command near Chancellorsville, and a spirited fight took place.

25. Much of the day's fighting was intended to keep the Federal troops occupied while Jackson's command made the twelve-mile-long flank march and got into position for the attack on Hooker's right flank.

26. Maj. Gen. Franz Sigel, an influential German immigrant who commanded this corps as part of John Pope's Army of Virginia during the 1862 Second Bull Run Campaign. Fight-

ing under Sigel was a matter of pride for the German immigrants who populated his command. "I fights mit Sigel" became a rallying cry for his men.

27. A single battery, the 1st Ohio Light Artillery, Battery I, made a stand and held off the Confederate onslaught long enough for a line of battle to be cobbled together. Its commander, Capt. Hubert Dilger, won the Medal of Honor for his stand. Earnest B. Furgurson, *Chancellorsville, 1863: The Souls of the Brave* (New York: Knopf, 1992), 183.

28. The Federal forces had formed a strong defensive perimeter around Chancellorsville. The bulk of the fighting was done by Couch's Second Corps and constituted the center portion of the line referred to by Smith in his letter. The left consisted of Maj. Gen. Daniel E. Sickles's Third Corps, which bore the brunt of the fighting at Hazel Grove. Ibid., 217.

29. In addition, Hooker was knocked senseless when he was struck on the head by a piece of roof that was knocked down by a Confederate artillery shell on the morning of May 3. Smith seems to describe this incident in his letter.

30. Army general in chief, Maj. Gen. Henry W. Halleck.

31. Maj. Gen. John Sedgwick, commanding the Union Sixth Corps.

32. Marye's Heights, scene of the worst of the fighting in the December 1862 Battle of Fredericksburg.

33. Furgurson, *Chancellorsville*, 364–65.

34. Clement Hoffman to Dear Mother, May 17, 1863, Letters to his Mother, Feb. 12, 1863–July 14, 1867, Clement Hoffman Letters, Civil War Roundtable Collection.

35. Rush was in poor health. He left the regiment on April 29, and it was thereafter commanded by Maj. Robert Morris, Jr. Perhaps the detachment of Smith's company to headquarters kept word of Rush's removal from reaching him in a timely fashion. Thus ended Richard Rush's dream of glory. He spent the rest of the war in an administrative position, commanding the Invalid Corps.

36. The lances were turned in on May 24 and the whole regiment was armed with Sharps carbines, single-shot breech-loading carbines with an effective range of about five hundred yards. They fired a .56-caliber ball and were rapid-firing. Chaplain Gracey noted, "The lance had been found to be illy adapted to cavalry service, as performed in the wooded country which we were called to operate." Gracey, *Annals*, 154–55.

37. OR, vol. 25, 1:1090; Christian Geisel to Dear Sister, May 20, 1863, Christian Geisel Letters.

38. Richard H. Rush to Col. Andrew J. Alexander, Apr. 25, 1863, Richard H. Rush service records, NA. Rush resigned his commission in the 6th Pennsylvania on September 30, 1863, after accepting a commission as colonel in the Invalid Corps, which he commanded for most of the rest of the war. Richard H. Rush to Lorenzo Thomas, Sept. 30, 1863, Richard H. Rush service records, NA; Alexander Biddle to Julia Biddle, June 21, 1863, Rush/Williams/Biddle Family Papers.

5. "The Sixth Pennsylvania Never Runs"

1. Heros von Borcke and Justus Siebert, *The Great Cavalry Battle of Brandy Station*, trans. Stuart T. Wright and F. D. Bridgewater (1893; reprint, Gaithersburg, Md.: Olde Soldier, 1976), 35.

2. *OR*, vol. 27, 1:18.

3. Ibid., 3:27–28.

4. Richard L. T. Beale, *History of the Ninth Virginia Cavalry in the War Between the States* (Richmond, Va.: B. F. Johnson, 1899), 85; John Buford to A. J. Alexander, June 13, 1863, Joseph Hooker Papers, Henry E. Huntington Library, San Marino, California.

5. Fairfax Downey, *Clash of Cavalry: The Battle of Brandy Station* (New York: David McKay, 1959), 103; Henry C. Whelan to James F. McQuesten, June 11, 1863, box 15, folder A, Joseph Hooker Papers.

6. Henry C. Whelan to Charles E. Cadwalader, June 11, 1863, Cadwalader Collection.

7. Lewis Miller to Col. Thomas, Sept. 13, 1863, Muster Rolls and Related Records, 1861–66, 70th Regiment–6th Cavalry, Records of the Department of Military Affairs, RG19, Pennsylvania State Archives, Harrisburg; Bates, *History* 6:1863.

8. Whelan to McQueston, June 11, 1863, and Charles J. Whiting to Theodore C. Bacon, June 12, 1863, box 15, folder A, Hooker Papers.

9. Whelan to Cadwalader, June 11, 1863, Cadwalader Papers; Frederick C. Newhall, "Presentation Address," *Dedication of the Monument of the 6th Pennsylvania Cavalry on the Battlefield of Gettysburg, October 14, 1888* (Philadelphia, 1889), 12–13.

10. Clement Hoffman to Dear Mother, June 23, 1863, Clement Hoffman Letters.

11. Smith refers here to the Battle of Brandy Station. He was mistaken about the location of the main fight. The bulk of the day's fighting actually took place in the fields surrounding Beverly's Ford, about six miles upriver from Kelly's Ford. He refers to Capt. Ulric Dahlgren, of Pleasonton's staff.

12. Smith refers to the melee for the Confederate artillery pieces at St. James Church.

13. Robert F. O'Neill, Jr., *The Cavalry Battles at Aldie, Middleburg, and Upperville; June 10–27, 1863: Small but Important Riots* (Lynchburg, Va.: H. E. Howard, 1993), 25.

14. Clement Hoffman to Dear Mother, June 23, 1863, Clement Hoffman Letters.

15. By this time, significant portions of Lee's army were already in Pennsylvania. For example, a column of Lt. Gen. Richard S. Ewell's Second Corps had already embarked on a raid to Harrisburg, and another column, under the command of Maj. Gen. Jubal A. Early, had passed through the small town of Gettysburg, marching east toward the town of York, thirty-two miles away.

16. Darius N. Couch had asked to be relieved of command of the Second Corps in disgust over Hooker's performance at Chancellorsville. He was then sent to command the Department of Pennsylvania, where he mustered the Pennsylvania militia forces to resist the Confederate advance toward Harrisburg.

17. Clement Hoffman to Dear Mother, July 5, 1863, Clement Hoffman Letters.

18. Taneytown, Maryland, about fourteen miles from the battlefield at Gettysburg.

19. The first day's battle took place to the north and west of the town of Gettysburg, where two brigades of Buford's cavalry held off a division of Confederate infantry long enough for two corps of Union infantry to arrive. Later that day, the Confederates drove the Union infantry back through the streets of the town to strategic high ground on Cemetery Hill just south of the town.

20. The Confederates launched a determined attack on the Union left flank late in the afternoon of July 2 and, after several desperate hours of fighting, nearly succeeded in capturing the critical hill known as Little Round Top.

21. That morning, the Confederate Second Corps launched a determined attack on the Federal right at Culp's Hill that also nearly succeeded.

22. Smith describes Pickett's Charge as the "high water mark" of the Confederacy. Smith is mistaken when he states that Longstreet personally led the attack. He did not.

23. Smith refers to the town of Boonsboro, Maryland, not far from the old Antietam battlefield, and the South Mountain range.

24. Clement Hoffman to Dear Mother, July 5, 1863, Clement Hoffman Letters.

25. The Widow Leister House, located near the Copse of Trees near the point of the Confederates' farthest advance during Pickett's Charge.

26. Capt. Emlen N. Carpenter, commander of Company E, 6th Pennsylvania Cavalry. Captured during 1864, Carpenter made a daring escape and eventually made his way back into Union lines.

27. By the eleventh, the Army of the Potomac had caught up to Lee's army, trapped along the banks of the flooded Potomac River near Williamsport, Maryland. A council of war was held that night and the army's corps commanders voted to attack. Smith was correct when he wrote this statement.

28. This is an interesting statement. When Smith filed his pension application in the 1880s, he stated that he began suffering rheumatism due to his service in the heavy rains after the end of the Battle of Gettysburg. See Smith's pension file, NA.

29. Newhall, "Dedication Address," 21.

30. This purported raid is not mentioned in the *Official Records*. What Smith referred to here is probably activity by Maj. John S. Mosby's partisan rangers.

31. Again, this is totally unsubstantiated and probably entirely myth. In fact, the historical record plainly indicates that Meade's own indecision, combined with the heavy casualties his army suffered at Gettysburg, are the primary reasons that a more vigorous pursuit was not made.

32. Actually, there were significant draft riots in New York City during July 1863, but there is no record of any taking place in Philadelphia during this time frame.

33. Upperville is a fair-sized town in the Loudoun Valley. A major cavalry battle was fought there on June 21, as the two foes jockeyed for position during the advance into Pennsylvania.

34. This was an engagement between Wesley Merritt's Regular Cavalry, supported by infantry of the Sixth Corps, and elements of Longstreet's Corps of the Army of Northern Virginia. See OR, vol. 27, 1:945.

35. The town of Salem, Virginia.

36. Interestingly, the regimental history states that Capt. Benoni Lockwood of Company H was in command of the regiment that day, not Hazeltine. Gracey, *Annals*, 194.

37. Smith refers to Brig. Gen. John Buford as commanding the division and wing of the Cavalry Corps of the Army of the Potomac; and the battery is probably Capt. Roger Preston Chew's battery of horse artillery, attached to the cavalry brigade of Brig. Gen. William E. "Grumble" Jones.

38. Lt. Edward Whiteford of Company H, who later became the regimental quartermaster.

39. This statement is consistent with Gracey's account of who commanded the regiment in the early days of August 1863.

40. Gracey, *Annals*, 194–95.

41. Actually, this occurred several days later, on August 15. Ibid., 195.

42. Ibid., 196; Christian Geisel to Dear Sister, Oct. 15, 1863, Christian Geisel Letters; Miller to Col. Thomas, Sept. 13, 1863, RG 19, Pennsylvania State Archives.

43. Most of the Army of the Potomac's Regular infantry was sent to New York City to quell the riots raging there against the draft being used by the Federal government to replenish the ranks of its field armies.

44. The troops referred to here are those forces sent to New York to quell the draft riots and then maintain peace.

45. There was some talk of sending a major portion of the Federal armies on an expedition to Mexico to remove the disliked regime of the French puppet emperor Maximillian, but this never happened.

46. Gracey, *Annals*, 199.

47. Ibid., 201.

48. Smith referred to twenty-nine year-old Brig. Gen. Wesley Merritt, who had commanded the Reserve Brigade since June 28, just before the Battle of Gettysburg. Merritt was widely considered to be a protégé of John Buford, under whom Merritt served in the old Second Dragoons before the outbreak of the Civil War.

49. After the conclusion of the Gettysburg campaign, the makeup of the Reserve Brigade was changed. The 6th U.S. Cavalry, which had been decimated during the campaign, was reassigned to be the headquarters escort for the Cavalry Corps. Its place was taken by the 19th New York Cavalry, also known as the 1st New York Dragoons.

50. Merritt apparently adopted this habit from John Buford, who first began calling the Lancers the Seventh Regulars after their stellar performance at Brandy Station on June 9.

51. Maj. Gen. Alfred Pleasonton, commanding the Cavalry Corps.

52. Theodore Sage service records, NA.

53. For more information about the aborted Mine Run Campaign, see Martin F. Graham and George F. Skoch, *Mine Run: A Campaign of Lost Opportunities, October 21, 1863–May 1, 1864*, 2d ed. (Lynchburg, Va.: H. E. Howard, 1987).

54. Gracey, *Annals*, 205, 207.

55. Capt. Emlen N. Carpenter to Dear. Mr. Henszey, Dec. 8, 1863, Alexander R. Chamberlain Collection.

56. Smith referred to an incident that occurred on December 4: "an alarm was created in camp at 3 o'clock in the morning in consequence of a reported attack upon our picket line. The regiment was quickly in line, and after an hour or two standing to horse, the men were allowed to tie their horses to their picket ropes, where they remained ready saddled until near noon." Gracey, *Annals*, 201–11.

57. Capt. Emlen N. Carpenter to Dear Mr. Henszey, Dec. 29, 1863, Alexander R. Chamberlain Collection.

58. It is not known what Smith referred to here. He spent most of his life as an upholsterer and had his own business before the war, but it is unclear if he is referring to that business.

59. Carpenter to Henszey, Dec. 29, 1863, Alexander R. Chamberlain Collection.

6. "BUT STILL THE COMMAND WAS FORWARD"

1. Gracey, Annals, 221.

2. John T. Baynes to Dear Stephen, Apr. 19, 1864, in The Life and Ancestry of John Thistlethwaite Baynes (1833–1891), comp. Richard C. Baynes (Irvine, Calif.: Richard C. Baynes, 1987), 38.

3. Gracey, Annals, 223; OR, vol. 33:164, 165.

4. Major William P. C. Treichel. According to Chaplain Gracey, the contingent from the 6th Pennsylvania Cavalry was commanded by Capt. Benoni Lockwood, not Major Treichel.

5. Brig. Gen. George A. Custer, commanding the Second Brigade, Third Division, Cavalry Corps. The Third Division was commanded by Brig. Gen. Hugh Judson Kilpatrick.

6. This may be Orange County Court House. It is somewhat unclear.

7. 1st U S Cavalry, also of the Reserve Brigade.

8. Smith means the Rivanna River.

9. Pennsylvanian Capt. Joseph Penrose Ash of the 5th U.S. Cavalry, who was killed in action in the cavalry battle near Todd's Tavern, Virginia, on May 8, 1864. Heitman, Historical Register 1:173.

10. Custer reported that there were two brigades of Confederate cavalry involved in this charge, including the brigade of Brig. Gen. Williams C. Wickham, along with another unidentified brigade, commanded in person by J. E. B. Stuart. Custer further reported that Stuart personally led a charge by the 1st and 5th Virginia Cavalry. OR, vol. 33:162.

11. Sgt. Samuel Wright of Philadelphia.

12. Actually, this is Burton's Ford over the Rapidan River.

13. This is really the Robinson River.

14. Contrabands were runaway slaves who often latched on to the coattails of the advancing Federal armies. Their presence was generally tolerated by the Yankee soldiers but not appreciated.

15. This is the infamous Kilpatrick/Dahlgren Raid, which was intended to liberate the Federal officers being held prisoner in Richmond's notorious Libby Prison. For further information see OR, vol. 33:182–224.

16. OR, vol. 33:163; Gracey, Annals, 227.

17. OR, vol. 33:163.

18. Theodore Sanford Garnett, Riding with Stuart: Reminiscences of an Aide-de-Camp, ed. Robert J. Trout (Shippensburg, Pa.: White Mane, 1994), 41–42. Garnett refers to Capt. Charles Gratton, Stuart's chief of ordnance.

19. OR, vol. 33:163.

20. Ibid., 783.

21. Bruce Catton, Grant Takes Command (Boston: Little, Brown, 1968), 163.

22. Grant summoned Sheridan to Washington with a request which stated "that the order relieving General Pleasonton be made at once. I will then direct General Meade to place the senior officer of the Cavalry Corps in command of it until General Sheridan arrives." *OR*, vol. 33:733.

23. E. R. Hagemann, ed., *Fighting Rebels and Redskins: Experiences of Army Life of Colonel George B. Sanford 1861–1892* (Norman: Univ. of Oklahoma Press, 1969), 224.

24. Smith was correct about this. Wright was discharged at the completion of his term of enlistment in September 1864.

25. Col. Alfred Gibbs. The Dragoons were also known as the 19th New York Cavalry, which joined the Reserve Brigade during the late fall of 1863.

26. Lt. Col. John H. McArthur, who came to the 6th Pennsylvania Cavalry from the 2d U.S. Cavalry. McArthur was ordered to report to the 5th U.S. Cavalry on February 3, 1862. Upon leaving the Lancers, McArthur was assigned to the 3d U.S. Cavalry, which served in the western theater. McArthur's service records, NA; Heitman, *Historical Register* 1:652.

27. Maj. C. Ross Smith, who eventually became the commanding officer of the 6th Pennsylvania Cavalry.

28. Maj. Robert Morris, Jr., captured at the June 9, 1863, Battle of Brandy Station, died in Libby Prison on August 12, 1863. Gracey, *Annals*, 198.

29. Maj. John H. Gardner resigned on February 5, 1863, as a result of disability. Ibid., 217.

30. Maj. J. Henry Hazeltine resigned on November 12, 1863, perhaps because of his disgrace at the August 1, 1863, fight at Brandy Station. Ibid., 218. Hazeltine's pension records indicate that he was honorably discharged in 1863. Perhaps he resigned to avoid the court-martial mentioned above. See Henry Hazeltine pension file, RG 15, NA.

31. Maj. Henry C. Whelan died on March 2, 1864, of an illness contracted due to his service in the field. Greatly loved by his men, Whelan was sorely missed. Gracey, *Annals*, 301–2.

32. Maj. Benoni Lockwood resigned March 15, 1864. Ibid., 302.

33. Maj. George E. Clymer of Reading, Pennsylvania, formerly commander of Company E, resigned his commission on February 5, 1863. Ibid., 215.

34. Until his promotion to major in late 1863, Starr was the commander of Smith's Company I.

35. This did not occur. The Cavalry Corps remained a distinct command until the end of the war.

36. *OR*, vol. 33:941; Christian Geisel to Dear Sister, May 3, 1864, Christian Geisel Letters; John T. Baynes to Dear Stephen, Apr. 19, 1864, in Richard C. Baynes, comp. *The Life and Ancestry of John Thistlethwaite Baynes (1833–1891)* (Irvine, Calif.: Richard C. Baynes, 1987), 38.

37. *OR*, vol. 36, 2:944–45.

38. Geisel to Dear Sister, May 3, 1864, Christian Geisel Letters. Shortly thereafter, in one of the battles around Richmond, Geisel received a severe wound in the shoulder. Captured by the Confederates, he was taken away. The wound eventually became infected, and Geisel died of disease, a lonely prisoner of war far from home.

39. Indeed the army's great movement began later that night. Smith's prediction was correct.

NOTES TO PAGES 120–127 161

40. This is Brig. Gen. Alfred T. A. Torbert, a New Jersey native and a former infantry officer.

41. The order was not countermanded. The cavalry moved just as ordered.

42. Jane Smith evidently took over the operation of a boarding house in Philadelphia during 1864.

43. May 4, 1864, entry, John P. Kepner Diary, Virginia Historical Society, Richmond.

44. Gordon C. Rhea, *The Battles for Spotsylvania Court House and the Road to Yellow Tavern, May 7–12, 1864* (Baton Rouge: Louisiana State Univ. Press, 1997), 30–37.

45. Ibid., 34; Fitzhugh Lee to Dear General, Dec. 20, 1866, Eleanor S. Brockenbrough Library, Museum of the Confederacy, Richmond.

46. Gracey, *Annals*, 235. Lt. William Kirk, the regimental commissary, was mortally wounded at Todd's Tavern on May 7. Capt. Emlen N. Carpenter was captured on May 7. After being held as a prisoner of war in South Carolina, Carpenter escaped and eventually made his way back to Federal lines. He eventually rejoined the regiment after his arduous experience. He was breveted major and lieutenant colonel for his gallant and meritorious service. Lt. Charles B. Coxe of Company K was severely wounded in the left shoulder also on May 7. See Kirk, Carpenter, and Coxe service records, NA.

47. *Philadelphia Inquirer*, May 10, 1863.

48. Christian Geisel to Dear Sister, May 17, 1864, Christian Geisel Letters; Gracey, *Annals*, 243–45.

49. OR, vol. 36, 1:805.

50. Soldiers often did this to lighten the load of what they carried into battle. For example, paper was seen as an unnecessary encumbrance.

51. Smith refers to Sheridan's Richmond raid.

52. Sgt. Lawrence Pennington, who was killed at great Battle of Trevilian Station on June 11, 1864.

53. William H. Rinehart. Interestingly, the muster roll lists Rinehart as being a private and does not reflect a promotion to sergeant.

54. Gracey, *Annals*, 258–59; Medal of Honor citation for Capt. Frank Furness, NA.

55. Fitzhugh Lee to Dear General, Dec. 20, 1866, Eleanor S. Brockenbrough Library; Memorandum of Maj. James D. Ferguson on the Virginia campaign, Jedediah Hotchkiss Papers, Manuscripts Division, Library of Congress, Washington, D.C.; OR, vol.36, 1:809.

56. Gracey, *Annals*, 263.

57. Ibid., 265.

58. Maj. Gen. David Hunter commanded a Federal force advancing up the Shenandoah Valley toward the vast Confederate supply depot at Lynchburg.

59. See Smith's service records, NA.

60. Gracey, *Annals*, 271.

61. In fact, the Confederates were. Lt. Gen. Jubal A. Early's Second Corps, renamed the Army of the Valley, advanced down the Shenandoah Valley, bypassed the Federal garrison at Harpers Ferry, and marched on the town of Frederick. A day-long delaying action was fought at the Battle of Monocacy on July 6, and Early then continued on to the outskirts of

Washington. He finally turned back on July 12 when he realized that the Federal defenses of the capital were too strong to attack with his small force.

62. On May 7, at the Battle of Todd's Tavern, Starr was shot in the face. The ball carried away part of his jaw bone, all of the teeth on the upper left side of his mouth, and all but one on the upper right side, leaving "a discharging wound." Amazingly, he was back on duty with the regiment just over a month later, having recuperated in Philadelphia. Starr served the remainder of the war and was eventually awarded a pension as a result of his wound. See James Starr pension file, RG 109, NA.

63. Smith's service records for summer 1864, NA.

64. OR, vol. 43, 1:94–95; Supplement to the Official Records of the Union and Confederate Armies, 100 vols. (Wilmington, N.C.: Broadfoot Publishing Co., 1997), ser. 2, vol. 68:813.

65. OR, vol. 43, 1:489; Philadelphia Inquirer, Nov. 4, 1864; OR, vol. 43, 2:52; Smith's service records and Detachment Muster-Out Roll, NA.

EPILOGUE

1. Gracey, Annals, 317, 324.

2. Ibid., 332–35.

3. Stephen Z. Starr, The Union Cavalry in the Civil War, 3 vols. (Baton Rouge: Louisiana State Univ. Press, 1976–80), 3:449.

4. Maj. Gen. Philip H. Sheridan to Samuel L. Gracey, Feb. 5, 1866, quoted in Gracey, Annals, I.

5. Addendum to the Dedication of the Monument of the 6th Penna. Cavalry on the Battlefield of Gettysburg, October 14, 1888 (Philadelphia, 1889), 38.

6. Thomas W. Smith pension file, reel 441, RG 109, NA.

7. Thomas W. Smith to Pensions Commissioner, Aug. 18, 1891, ibid.

8. Record Proof of Marriages, Births and Deaths of Thomas W. Smith, ibid.

9. Thomas W. Smith to Pensions Commissioner, Aug. 18, 1891, and Physician's Affidavit of Joseph Hancock, M.D., ibid.

10. Smith to Pensions Commissioner, Aug. 18, 1891, ibid.

11. Affidavit of Mary A. Smith, ibid.

12. Original Invalid Claim, ibid.

13. Philadelphia Press, Apr. 28, 1896.

14. Thomas W. Smith death certificate, Smith pension file, NA. Today, the gravestones from Monument Cemetery lie under a bridge abutment for the Betsy Ross Bridge over the Delaware River. The bodies were removed and reburied, but many of the grave markers were left behind, and many of them lie in unmarked graves. The location of Tom Smith's grave is unknown, a tragedy in itself.

Bibliography

NEWSPAPERS

National Tribune
Philadelphia Inquirer
Philadelphia Press
Philadelphia Public Ledger
Reading Eagle
Reading Times

MANUSCRIPT COLLECTIONS

Eleanor Brockenbrough Library, Museum of the Confederacy, Richmond, Virginia
    Fitzhugh Lee Papers
Chester County Historical Society, Chester, Pennsylvania
    Family Newspaper Clippings Files for Abraham Wanger
Historical Society of Pennsylvania, Philadelphia, Pennsylvania
    Cadwalader Collection, Collection No. 1454
    Thomas W. Smith Letters
    J. K. Stoddard Collection, Correspondence of the Newhall Family, Collection
        No. 1199
    Wright Family Papers, Collection No. 2096
Henry E. Huntington Library, San Marino, California
    Joseph Hooker Papers
Richard Lewis Collection, Lexington, Virginia
    Oliver Willets Letters
Library of Congress, Manuscripts Division, Washington, D.C.
    Jedediah Hotchkiss Papers
Pennsylvania State Archives, Harrisburg, Pennsylvania
    Christian Geisel Letters
    Samuel P. Bates Papers
    RG 19, Muster Rolls and Related Records, 1861–65, Seventieth Regiment-Sixth
        Cavalry
Rosenbach Museum, Philadelphia, Pennsylvania
    Rush/Williams/Biddle Family Papers, series 4, box 30
University of Michigan, Clements Library, Ann Arbor, Michigan
    Edgar H. Klemroth Papers

U.S. Army Military History Institute, Carlisle Barracks, Pennsylvania
    Alexander R. Chamberlain Collection
    Civil War Times Illustrated Collection
    Harrisburg Civil War Roundtable Collection
    Clement Hoffman Letters
    Lewis Leigh Collection
    Spanish/American War Survey, Civil War box
    Wiley Sword Collection
Virginia Historical Society, Richmond, Virginia
    John Price Kepner Diary for 1864
Wisconsin State Archives, Madison, Wisconsin
    Sue Clark Knight Papers

Published Sources

Agassiz, George R., ed. *Meade's Headquarters, 1863–1865: Letters of Colonel Theodore Lyman from the Wilderness to Appomattox.* 1922. Reprint, Lincoln: University of Nebraska Press, 1994.

Arnold, Lt. Col. Abraham K. "The Cavalry at Gaines' Mill." *Journal of the United States Cavalry Association* 2 (1889).

Bates, Samuel P. *History of Pennsylvania Volunteers, 1861–1865.* 3 vols. Harrisburg, Pa.: B. Singerly, 1869.

Baynes, Richard C., comp. *The Life and Ancestry of John Thistlethwaite Baynes (1833–1891).* Irvine, Calif.: Richard C. Baynes, 1987.

Beale, Richard L. T. *History of the Ninth Virginia Cavalry in the War Between the States.* Richmond, Va.: B. F. Johnson Publishing, 1889.

Bearss, Ed, and Chris Calkins. *The Battle of Five Forks.* 2d ed. Lynchburg, Va.: H. E. Howard, Inc., 1985.

Bigelow, John, Jr. *Chancellorsville.* New York: Knoecky & Konecky, 1995.

Catton, Bruce. *Grant Takes Command.* Boston: Little, Brown & Co., 1968.

Congdon, James A. *Congdon's Cavalry Compendium: Containing Instructions for Non-Commissioned Officers and Privates in the Cavalry Service.* Philadelphia: J. B. Lippincott & Co., 1864.

Conrad, W. P., and Ted Alexander. *When War Passed This Way.* Greencastle, Pa.: Lilian S. Besore Library, 1982.

Cooke, Philip St. George. "The Cavalry at Gaines Mill." In Johnson and Buel, *Battles and Leaders* 2:344–46.

————. *Cavalry Tactics: or Regulations for the Instruction, Formations, and Movements of the Cavalry of the Army and Volunteers of the United States.* Philadelphia: J. B. Lippincott & Co., 1862.

Couch, Darius N. "The Chancellorsville Campaign." In Johnson and Buel, *Battles and Leaders* 3:154–71.

Crowninshield, Benjamin W. "Sheridan at Winchester." *Atlantic Monthly* 42 (1878).

Davis, Sidney Morris. *Common Soldier, Uncommon War: Life as a Civil War Cavalryman.* Edited by Charles F. Cooney. Bethesda, Md.: SMD Group, 1994.

Downey, Fairfax. *Clash of Cavalry: The Battle of Brandy Station.* New York: David McKay, 1959.

Egle, William H., ed. *Andrew Gregg Curtin: His Life and Services.* Philadelphia: Avil Printing Co., 1895.

Foote, Shelby. *The Civil War: A Narrative.* 3 vols. New York: Vintage Books, 1986.

Furgurson, Earnest B. *Chancellorsville, 1863: The Souls of the Brave.* New York: Knopf & Sons, 1992.

Gallagher, Gary W., ed. *Chancellorsville: The Battle and Its Aftermath.* Chapel Hill: University of North Carolina Press, 1996.

Garnett, Theodore Sanford. *Riding with Stuart: Reminiscences of an Aide-de-Camp.* Edited by Robert J. Trout. Shippensburg, Pa.: White Mane, 1994.

Gracey, Samuel L. *Annals of the 6th Pennsylvania Cavalry.* 1868. Reprint, Lancaster, Ohio: VanBerg Publishing, 1996.

Graham, Martin F., and George F. Skoch. *Mine Run: A Campaign of Lost Opportunities, October 21, 1863–May 1, 1864.* 2d ed. Lynchburg, Va.: H. E. Howard Co., 1987.

Grant, Ulysses S. *Personal Memoirs of U.S. Grant.* 2 vols. New York, 1885–86.

Grimsley, Daniel A. *Battles in Culpeper County, Virginia, 1861–1865.* Orange, Va.: Green Publishers, Inc., 1900.

Hagemann, E. R., ed. *Fighting Rebels and Redskins: Experiences In Army Life of Colonel George B. Sanford 1861–1892.* Norman: University of Oklahoma Press, 1969.

Hall, Clark B. "The Battle of Brandy Station." *Civil War Times Illustrated* (May/June 1990).

———. "Buford at Brandy Station." *Civil War* 8 (July/August 1990).

Heitman, Francis E. *Historical Register and Dictionary of the U.S. Army.* 2 vols. Washington, D.C.: GPO, 1904.

Henderson, William D. *The Road to Bristoe Station: Campaigning with Lee and Meade, August 1–October 20, 1863.* 2d ed. Lynchburg, Va: H. E. Howard Co., 1987.

History of the First Troop Philadelphia City Cavalry, From Its Organization November 17th, 1774 to Its Centennial Anniversary November 17th, 1874. Trenton, N.J.: Trenton-Princeton, 1874.

Johnson, Robert U., and Clarence C. Buel, eds. *Battles and Leaders of the Civil War.* 4 vols. New York: Century, 1884–1901.

Longacre, Edward G. *Mounted Raids of the Civil War.* Lincoln: University of Nebraska Press, 1975.

McClellan, Henry B. *The Life and Campaigns of Major-General J. E. B. Stuart, Commander of the Cavalry of the Army of Northern Virginia.* Boston: Houghton, Mifflin & Co., 1885.

McDonald, William N. *A History of the Laurel Brigade.* Baltimore, Md.: Sun Job Printing Office, 1907.

Matter, William D. *If It Takes All Summer: The Battle for Spotsylvania.* Chapel Hill: University of North Carolina Press, 1988.

Meade, George G. *The Life and Letters of George Gordon Meade.* 2 vols. New York: Charles Scribner's Sons, 1913.

Montgomery, Norton L. *History of Berks County, Pennsylvania.* Philadelphia: Everts, Peck & Richards, 1886.

Moore, Frank, ed. *Rebellion Record: A Diary of American Events with Documents, Narratives, Illustrative Incidents, Poetry, Etc.* 11 vols. and supplement. New York, 1861–68.

Morris, Roy, Jr. *Sheridan: The Life and Wars of General Phil Sheridan.* New York: Crown Publishers, Inc., 1992.

Neese, George M. *Three Years in the Confederate Horse Artillery.* Dayton, Ohio: Morningside, 1988.

Nevins, Allan, ed. *A Diary of Battle: The Personal Journals of Colonel Charles S. Wainwright, 1861–1865.* 1962. Reprint, Gettysburg, Pa.: Stan Clark, 1994.

Newhall, Frederick C. "Presentation Address." Dedication of the Monument of the 6th Pennsylvania Cavalry on the Battlefield of Gettysburg, October 14, 1888. Philadelphia, 1889.

———. *With General Sheridan in Lee's Last Campaign, by a Staff Officer.* Philadelphia: J. B. Lippincott & Co., 1866.

O'Neill, Robert F., Jr. *The Cavalry Battles of Aldie, Middleburg, and Upperville, June 10–27, 1863: Small but Important Riots.* Lynchburg, Va.: H. E. Howard Co., 1993.

Pleasonton, Alfred. "The Successes and Failures of Chancellorsville." In Johnson and Buel, *Battles and Leaders* 3:172–82.

Porter, Horace. *Campaigning with Grant.* Bloomington: University of Indiana Press, 1951. *Supplement to the Official Records of the Union and Confederate Armies.* 100 vols. Wilmington, N.C.: Broadfoot Publishing Co., 1997.

Rhea, Gordon F. *The Battles for Spotsylvania Court House and the Road to Yellow Tavern, May 7–12, 1864.* Baton Rouge: Louisiana State University Press, 1997.

———. *The Battle of the Wilderness: May 5–6, 1864.* Baton Rouge: Louisiana State University Press, 1994.

Sears, Stephen W. *Landscape Turned Red: The Battle of Antietam.* New York: Ticknor & Fields, 1983.

———. *To the Gates of Richmond: The Peninsula Campaign.* New York: Ticknor & Fields, 1992.

Starr, Stephen Z. *The Union Cavalry in the Civil War.* 3 vols. Baton Rouge: Louisiana State University Press, 1976–80.

Swinton, William. *Campaigns of the Army of the Potomac.* New York, 1882.

Taylor, Frank H. *Philadelphia in the Civil War.* Philadelphia, 1879.

Todd, Frederick P., and Harry G. Larter. "6th Pennsylvania Cavalry (Rush's Lancers), 1862." *Military Collector & Historian* 6 (1954). *A Trooper's Adventure in the War for the Union.* New York: Hurst & Co., 1863.

Trudeau, Noah Andre. *Bloody Road South: The Wilderness to Cold Harbor, May–June 1864.* Boston: Little, Brown & Co., 1989.

Von Borcke, Heros. *Memoirs of the Confederate War for Independence*. Philadelphia: J. B. Lippincott & Co., 1867.

Von Borcke, Heros, and Justus Siebert. *The Great Cavalry Battle of Brandy Station*. Translated by Stuart T. Wright and F. D. Bridgewater. 1893. Reprint, Gaithersburg, Md.: Olde Soldier, 1976. *The War of the Rebellion: A Compilation of the Official Records of the Union and Confederate Armies*. Ser. 1, 128 vols. Washington, D.C.: GPO, 1880–1901.

Warner, Ezra J. *Generals in Blue*. Baton Rouge: Louisiana State University Press, 1964.

Watson, George William. *The Last Survivor: The Memoirs of George William Watson*. Edited by Brian Stuart Kesterson. Washington, W.Va.: Night Hawk Press, 1993.

Waugh, John C. *Class of 1846*. New York: Warner Books, 1994.

Wells, Edward L. *Hampton and His Cavalry in '64*. Richmond, Va.: B. F. Johnson Publishing Co., 1899.

———. *A Sketch of the Charleston Light Dragoons from the Earliest Formation of the Corps*. Charleston, S.C.: Lucas, Richardson & Co., 1888.

Wert, Jeffry D. *From Winchester to Cedar Creek: The Shenandoah Campaign of 1864*. Carlisle, Pa.: South Mountain Press, 1987.

Wittenberg, Eric J. "An Analysis of the Buford Manuscripts." *The Gettysburg Magazine* 15 (July 1996).

———. "John Buford in the Gettysburg Campaign." *The Gettysburg Magazine* 11 (July 1994).

———. "Merritt's Regulars on South Cavalry Field: Oh, What Could Have Been." *The Gettysburg Magazine* 16 (January 1997).

Woodward, Joseph Janvier. *Outline of the Chief Camp Diseases of the United States Armies*. Philadelphia: J. B. Lippincott, 1863.

UNPUBLISHED SOURCES

Harper, Douglas, comp. "Index of Civil War Soldiers and Sailors from Chester County, Pennsylvania." Chester County Historical Society, Chester, Pennsylvania.

O'Neill, Robert F., Jr. "The Federal Cavalry in the Peninsula Campaign." Unpublished manuscript, 1995.

Thiele, T. F. "The Evolution of Cavalry in the American Civil War, 1861–1865." Ph.D. diss. University of Michigan, 1951.

Index

"We Have It Damn Hard Out Here"
was designed by Diana Dickson,
composed in 10.5-point Quadraat leaded 3 points
on a Macintosh Power PC system using QuarkXPress
at The Book Page, Inc.;
printed by sheet-fed offset lithography
on 50-pound Lyons Falls Turin Book natural stock
(an acid-free, totally chlorine-free paper),
Smyth sewn and bound over binder's boards in Arrestox B cloth,
and wrapped with dust jackets printed in three colors
on 100-pound enamel stock finished with
polypropylene matte film lamination
by Thomson-Shore, Inc.;
and published by
The Kent State University Press
KENT, OHIO 44242